ROWING INTO THE SON

To Lorraine,

Keep the Round side Down!

♡ Jordan E Hess

JORDAN HANSSEN

ROWING INTO THE SON

Four Young Men Crossing the North Atlantic

THE MOUNTAINEERS BOOKS

THE MOUNTAINEERS BOOKS

is the nonprofit publishing arm of The Mountaineers,
an organization founded in 1906 and dedicated to the exploration,
preservation, and enjoyment of outdoor and wilderness areas.

1001 SW Klickitat Way, Suite 201, Seattle, WA 98134

First edition, 2012

Manufactured in the United States of America

Copy Editor: Beth Chapple
Cover Design: McGuire Barber Design
Book Design: Peggy Egerdahl
Cartographer: John Barnett, 4 Eyes Design
All photographs by the author unless otherwise noted.

Frontispiece: *Greg and Jordan row over swells.*

Tales of Brave Ulysses lyrics © Martin Sharp and Eric Clapton, used with permission.

Library of Congress Cataloging-in-Publication Data
Hanssen, Jordan.
  Rowing into the son : four young men crossing the North Atlantic / by Jordan Hanssen.
    p. cm.
  ISBN 978-1-59485-635-8 (pbk) — ISBN 978-1-59485-636-5 (ebook)
  1. Rowing—North Atlantic Ocean. I. Title.
  GV791.H35 2012
  797.12'3091631—dc23
                                    2012018925

ISBN (paperback): 978-1-59485-635-8
ISBN (ebook): 978-1-59485-636-5

SUSTAINABLE
FORESTRY
INITIATIVE

Certified Chain of Custody
Promoting Sustainable Forestry

www.sfiprogram.org
SFI-01268

SFI label applies to the text stock

For my family

—ᴎᴧᴧ—

Fit out a ship with twenty oars, the best in sight,
sail in quest of news of your long lost father.

—Athena to Telemachus, son of Odysseus
(from Homer's *The Odyssey*)

Contents

Author's Note

Eighteen months to prepare to row across the ocean, seventy-two days at sea, and six years to write a book about it—I suppose that sums it up.

This is not the unbiased and omniscient history of the 2006 North Atlantic rowing race. It's my story of what happened on the boat. Sixteen men left New York with the intention of rowing across the ocean and each of them went through some significant transformation. I wish I had the means to do all their stories justice. As it is, I must stick to what I know.

Contemporary adventurers have a great deal of resources at their fingertips. To distill my story into what you have in your hands I sifted through roughly one thousand emails exchanged while at sea. I looked at some one hundred hours of video footage. I also used our logbook, blog posts, and the generous time of several characters in the book. For details on George Harbo and Frank Samuelsen's epic first ocean row in 1896 I referred to *Daring the Sea* by David W. Shaw. Any mistakes in the retelling are entirely my own.

The book contains about sixty named characters. This represents less than 10 percent of the people involved with the ocean rowing project in some shape or form. I wish I could name them all. Unfortunately all I have room for is a very incomplete list of people and organizations I would like to name and thank who are not mentioned in the book: Kyle Putnam, Tom O'Brien, Don Kennedy, SYC Foundation, Deneva Flath, Pat Boyle, Geoff Douthwaite, Craig Hill, Michael King, Gareth Etchells, Jeff Howell, Loyal Moore,

Paul Payton, Marina Cofer-Wildsmith, Jim Scroggs, Charlie Vanderburg, Karl Mundt, the Board of the Lake Washington Rowing Club, the Board of Sound Rowers and Paddlers, Foss Waterway, Seaport, Rite in the Rain, Pat Sanford, Kokatat Watersports Wear, Lynden Freight, Kaenon Polarized, Jetboil, Tacoma Yacht Club, Port Townsend Yacht Club, and many others.

The participation of so many, and their belief in us, continues to humble me. I speak for the crew when I say we are profoundly grateful for their efforts in helping us realize this experience. Something about our decision to row the ocean made others see the very best in us. That faith dared us to try and live up to that ideal—sometimes we got close.

A photo or two starts each chapter. Obviously the shots from inside the boat were taken by the crew. Other photos can be attributed to Jim Wood, and the original artwork can be attributed to the students at West Woodland Elementary, made after a visit to the school before the trip. A very special thanks to Erinn J. Hale. She went the distance with us, capturing hundreds of hauntingly accurate images. A day of writing did not go by that I looked at them for inspiration to tell my story.

I would like to thank my agent, Anne Depue, for her willingness to go above and beyond her job description to coach a clueless first-time author through the book writing process, as well as her continual belief in a story that has taken years to come to print. I thank Kate Rogers, Editor in Chief at The Mountaineers Books, for taking a chance on this project, and her introduction to my editor, Amy Smith Bell, who was a joy to work with as she took my jumble of words and helped me build a story.

Last and most certainly not least I want to thank my parents, Eve Hanssen-Wood and Jim Wood, and my brother Douglas Wood for their love and incredible editorial support. I also want to thank Kim Gallagher, Karen Johnson, Dave Robertson, and Ben Martin, who either over a period of many months or at the last minute and with little notice went the distance through the book's very many edits.

Writing this book allowed me to relive the adventure, and that was a privilege. I did my best to be fair to all of us, and hopefully my love and admiration for the men on the crew is apparent. I hope you enjoy it.

Prologue

Dylan and Greg rowed at twenty-six strokes a minute. Each swing of the oar clunked as it changed direction, sending a rustle of bubbles swirling past the hull. It was the sound of progress. Anything but steady advancement was cause for concern. Sun burned off the last cool vestiges of night. Brad was inside the cabin. He was not a morning person, but today he seemed especially morose. I sat on deck entertaining the rowers and enjoying bites of plain lumpy oatmeal. Greg and Dylan rowed steadily, feigning polite interest in my retelling of *Around the World in Eighty Days*. Anything that might divert our glum thoughts from the still-unfound Gulf Stream current was a welcome distraction. We considered the famous current critical to our success—so much so that we gave it a soul. Dylan was convinced that it was purposely testing our will to row across this ocean.

The Gulf Stream is born from equatorial water driven by the sun's heat and east wind into the Gulf of Mexico before it starts its journey up the eastern seaboard of North America. Somewhere between the latitude of Charlotte and New York, the sixty-mile-wide current meanders toward northern Europe at up to five knots, throwing off equally strong and constantly changing eddies 150 miles long and as wide as the stream itself. On the pixelated thermal maps downloaded via satellite phone to our onboard computer, the Gulf Stream looked like a breath of red and yellow fire streaming into the cold blue North Atlantic. This natural phenomenon is the reason that London has a warmer winter than New York, even though it is more than

Our mascot, Rex

750 miles closer to the North Pole. Harnessing its power would fling us toward our final race destination in England. Getting caught in the eddy would slow any boat, especially one without engine or sails.

Seventeen days into the trip—with a tropical storm, lightning, and a stampede of dolphins under our belt, but no sign of our swift current—an even larger problem was about to reveal itself. After I finished my two-hour turn at the oars, sleep remained elusive, my body unable to wind down. I stared up at the note duct-taped by Brad to the white bulkhead and read it for the hundredth time. "Courage is starting the race with no end in sight." It was from Brad's mother.

Brad shifted uncomfortably next to me in the cabin. He spoke clearly, but his meaning didn't register at first. "What was that?" I asked.

"I need to talk to you about the food."

GREENLAND

NORTH
ATLANTIC OCEAN

CANADA

NEWFOUNDLAND

Gulf of St. Lawrence

NEW YORK

UNITED
STATES

1

2

3

4

5

70°W

60°W

50°W

Arctic Circle

ICELAND

60°N

2006 NORTH ATLANTIC
GUINNESS RECORD CROSSING

1 > 6.10 Leave New York harbor.

2 > 6.14 Dolphin stampede

3 > 6.15 Tropical Storm Alberto

4 > 6.27 Brad tells us we did not bring enough food. Find Gulf Stream.

5 > 7.07 *Sula* comes to visit for the last time.

6 > 7.10 Pod of 40 pilot whales accosts boat.

7 > 7.24 Greg gets sick. Down to 3 rowers

8 > 8.04 Jordan's 24th birthday

9 > 8.16 Near collision with Freighter *CGM Matisse*

10 > 8.18 Cross finish line.

11 > 8.19 Sight land.

12 > 8.20 Make landfall in Falmouth.

IRELAND

ENGLAND

50°N

9 10 12

FALMOUTH

11

8

FRANCE

7

SPAIN

40°N

AZORES

30°W   20°W   10°W   AFRICA

PART ONE

*Leaving Liberty Landing Marina for the starting line
just off the Statue of Liberty* (Erinn J. Hale)

—⁓—

Chapter 1

To the Sea

The sparkling waves are calling you
to kiss their white-laced lips.
—Cream, "Tales of Brave Ulysses"

Race Day 1: June 10, 10:45 AM

Wagner's "Ride of the Valkyries" blasted from speakers built into the rowboat's hull. I yanked for my life on two ten-foot oars.

"Jordan, I hate to say this, but Rex is bowing," said my teammate Greg. Like me, he wore child-sized neon-orange water wings in playful insubordination to our epic task.

I sat in the bow seat, facing backward, the normal position in a rowboat. Twisting my neck between strokes, I looked at our plastic dinosaur mascot. Indeed, he had lost his balance. Fortunately Rex's feet had been duct-taped to the bulkhead. A five-story black steel bow of a freighter filled the rest of my vision. Greg pointed to it, steering us resolutely toward the huge ship in a real-life David and Goliath game of chicken. *Finally*, I thought, *a moment in my life worthy of Wagner.*

I looked at Greg and corrected him. "Rex," I said, grunting out the words between strokes, "is bowing to the Atlantic."

607 Days till Race

"ONE LIFE, LIVE IT," beckoned the race poster from the boathouse wall. It had been up for a week. The slogan was augmented by the image of two men, bronzed by the sun and taut from Sisyphean labor. Casually aware and by all appearances unworried, they rode a strange rowing craft down a house-sized wave. The poster had been the subject of amusement all week—no one expected anyone to take it seriously. Who the hell would row across the ocean in a twenty-nine-foot fiberglass boat? And why?

Day 1, 10:48 AM

Wind blew at a steady twenty knots west over the sparkling brown Hudson River. Waves thudded against the windward side of the massive steel hull ahead of us, sending spray high into the air. Greg set his jaw in concentration, eyes invisible behind polarized glasses, and pointed his hand toward the freighter's bow less than a hundred yards away. Lady Liberty loomed above with stoic disinterest at the race unfolding below. Her colossal torch held aloft, this time not in greeting but as a bon voyage to the first four native sons to cross the proverbial pond in a rowboat.

"Hard port!" cried Greg.

I rotated my right foot on the steering column. Zephyr himself gripped our exposed broadside and pushed our craft diagonally toward the oncoming steel bow. Brad and I responded with firm starboard strokes. The ninety-foot beam of the freighter—three times the length of our boat—continued to approach.

596 Days till Race

It was 5:10 AM on a Thursday in late October. Fall had settled in Seattle, and Greg and I stretched on the cold gray carpet of the Lake Washington Rowing Club.

"Would you ever consider it?" I asked, nodding to the poster on the boathouse wall.

"No, but I think it's a big idea," he said. Gregory Joseph Spooner had an athletic all-American look and a large chin that seemed to lend him some natural credibility in all things sporting. At twenty-six he was four years my senior. Both of us had rowed for the University of Puget Sound a few years before but never in the same boat. The past two weeks were the first time we had rowed together. We had a similar goal: to pursue rowing postcollegiately to find out if our fastest was good enough to get on the US national rowing team.

I saw him considering the question despite our casual acquaintance. Besides, he had just been fired from his real estate job—what else was he going to do?

Day 1, 10:49 AM

Our craft cleared the bow of the freighter, exposing eight hundred feet of flat water that had been sheltered by its massive bulk. Getting this close to a vessel of this size would have been suicide had it not been anchored. Six hundred feet behind us, three nearly identical rowboats crashed through the water trying to catch us. Hard strokes, lightened by the tailwind and made more effective on the unnatural patch of calm water, allowed massive gains over our all-British competition.

I thought of the last line on the poster on the boathouse wall: "No Rowing Experience Required." Naturally this appeared in much smaller font. Now eight soldiers and four police officers—all accomplished veterans—chased us toward flat water. They were not trained oarsmen but what rowing skill they lacked, they made up for in toughness. They were fueled by a desire we could not share: these men were rowing home. I did not know if the tongue-in-cheek claim that our competitors had killed men with their bare hands had any truth, but the soldiers had been to Iraq. I was much happier to be in this kind of armed contest.

Two weeks earlier, it was obvious as we sized up everyone's vessels in the Liberty Landing boatyard that my crew had spent the most time developing very specific—and what we hoped was faster—ocean rigging. These boats were not sleek, flat-water racing craft. They were the burly monster trucks of rowboats. A big engine in the form of a pair of strong people would move each one. So far, our technique was proving itself: ten minutes into the transatlantic race, we were beating the British on American water. Now all we had to do is keep it up all the way to Falmouth, Cornwall, on the coast of England.

Day 1, 10:52 AM

Flat water helped us open our lead to an eighth of a mile. In my other rowing races, this would have meant victory, but over the ocean the distance was a drop in the bucket. The six-mile sprint from the Statue of Liberty to the Verrazano-Narrows Bridge was not our idea; at least I don't think so. However, the week before, after a long day at the humid, muddy boatyard finishing up last-minute details, the sixteen aspiring ocean rowers were in the mood to posture. The beer had flowed freely and cheaply at the bar next to the marina. Who had proposed this unofficial race to the edge of the Atlantic was anybody's guess.

593 Days till Race

"If I were going to row across the ocean, would you row with me?" After a no from Greg a few days earlier, I rehearsed the question several times before approaching my next prospective teammate: Bradley Charles Vickers. If anyone I knew would say yes, it would be Brad. Like me, he was a bit of a romantic. His rowing odyssey started like many others at a small Division III school desperate for numbers to fill its boats: through coercion, begging, and intimidation by classmates. The mischievous six-foot-six freshman with mantis-like appendages easily stood out at an activities fair. Sidling up on either side of him, my teammate and I showered him with compliments and good-natured threats while firmly guiding Brad toward the rowing booth. Rowing had proved a good fit for him—he was now rowing for his fourth year, three of those spent with me.

Rain pattered on the hood of Brad's jacket, audible through his cell phone. At twenty-one he was a year younger than me and still a college senior. I had reached him outside, parking cars at the University of Washington to help raise money for the crew team. There was a long silence on the other end of the line. Three years of rowing together had produced a strong bond between us. Was it this strong? I imagined him rolling over the idea as one might inspect a fine cigar.

"Send me what information you have, and we'll talk."

Day 1, 11:06 AM

The *Excalibur* listed ten degrees to port. The 135-foot mega yacht was packed over capacity with almost two hundred family members, friends, and significant others related to the rowers who had just started their race across the Atlantic. Among them were the three women of Women Helping Ocean Adventure Racing Northwest—or WHOAR Northwest, a crudely playful title Greg's girlfriend, Betsy, had coined for herself and the other girlfriends, Rebecca and Emily. Their support throughout the past eighteen months had kept us human. They had fund-raised, packed food, and in my girlfriend Rebecca's case, actually outfitted hardware on the boat.

Forty-five minutes earlier, Kathy Minnis, the producer of our film documentary, had nervously watched the young women say good-bye to us on the dock from her spot on the *Excalibur*'s gangplank. A huge crowd was lined up. The purser was anxious about overfilling the boat and threatened to not let anyone else on board. Kathy waved her camera and press pass wildly in the purser's face. "She's a fiancée, she's a fiancée, and she's a fiancée," she said loudly, pointing to our girlfriends in the back of the line. Just like that, Kathy had upgraded our relationship statuses.

586 Days till Race

A week after I had proposed the ocean row I met Brad at a coffee shop at the university. It was clear from the printouts and notes he'd brought along that he had been thinking. For eight hours straight we talked of planning, logistics, and commitment. He was in.

We needed two more teammates. I felt there was more to Greg's no than he had let on. Perhaps he was still a possibility. Assuming I was right, that left one more space to fill. We needed someone smart, good with his hands, and practical. Most important, this person needed to believe in rowing across the ocean.

571 Days till Race

Enter Dylan Madrone LeValley—same age and year in school as Brad. Even at a Division III school, Dylan—at a barrel-chested five foot ten—was considered a short rower. Whatever he lacked in height, he made up with a cast-iron work ethic and consistent performance. This combination made him one of the first seats determined in the varsity boat. Dylan had a knack for the outdoors and a reputation for handiness that manifested itself in his strong, pawlike hands. He also liked to win but rarely admitted it. He was an intensely practical person, and I had my doubts that he would be interested.

"What do you think of our proposition?" Brad had approached Dylan a few days earlier and was curious to see if the idea had sprouted. "You still want to row an ocean?"

Dylan watched his bagel go by on the conveyer belt of the temperamental industrial toaster at the school's cafeteria. He sighed and grabbed the now blackened piece of bread. With his Northern Californian brogue, he said, "I'm just trying not to get too excited about it." His mother would later call the trip "the dumbest idea" she had ever heard.

—◊◊◊—

That night I called Greg. "We have a team," I blurted. He was silent. "I'm serious, Greg, we could totally do this. Hear me out." Dylan had officially joined us, and I explained what Brad and I had found out about sponsorship and timelines.

"I'll help you guys in an advisory capacity, something like a manager," he finally conceded.

I didn't buy it. "Do you seriously believe that you would put any work into this at all, make it to New York with a boat ready, and not want to row across the ocean?" He didn't take the bait. "I swear, Greg, if we get that far, you would break someone's leg to get in that boat."

Day 1, 11:39 AM

The Verrazano-Narrows Bridge towered above us. What speed the other boats had found on the leeward side of the freighter had not been enough to move into our lead. The *Excalibur* exposed its broadside once more. We caught the last sight of our loved ones on this side of the ocean.

Dylan emerged from the cabin. He joined Greg on deck, and the pair replaced Brad and me, starting the unending rowing cycle that would dominate our lives for months.

547 Days till Race

Greg didn't have to break anyone's leg. We needed to make a final decision by New Year's. Everyone would be responsible for a quarter of the twelve-hundred-dollar race entry fee. Shortly I would know who was in and who was out. Dylan and Brad each gave me a check. Greg sold me his old oars, bartering his way into a yes. It was done. We were OAR Northwest, and in eighteen months we would start our race across the ocean.

———

There were many things we could do together. Why row an ocean? Why row at all? Elegant precision teamwork is what is observed from shore—but a row, especially a rowing race, is a rhythmic, primal, meditative ordeal. Done right, the only casualties are the fears each rower brings into the boat. A race starts with anticipation of the pain. It arrives with a choice: to push forward with complete disregard for the body or to hold back. To me, the act of rowing is a metaphor for trust. To pull hardest is to have blind faith that the other rowers are doing the same. At the finish line, if faith has been kept, a cathartic fire has blazed through each rower. It's addictive. It's what connected the four of us.

Rowing is a religion unto itself, and our parish church was American Lake, south of Tacoma, Washington. Our holy man was Chief Red Beard (aka Coach Mike Hagmann) of the University of Puget Sound, who delivered sermons through his bullhorn on cold mornings. Nicknamed for his auburn goatee, Hagmann inspired several years of novice rowers with tribal loyalty for the sport and each other. According to him, the boat went or it did not. It was a matter of faith.

Dylan, Brad, and I had shared victory and defeat. Rowing built trust—enough to entertain the thought of spending months together in this dangerous environment. Greg was a few years ahead of us, and save the few months I had rowed with him recently, none of us knew him that well. He had been one of Chief Red Beard's rowers, though. This was enough for me.

Day 1, Noon

The *Excalibur* was already well on its way back to port. Aboard a small yellow skiff, Todd Soliday brought the camera down from his shoulder as the small boat turned back into the harbor. Less than six weeks ago our team had walked into the film company, Flying Spot Entertainment, where Todd worked with Kathy. He thought our idea was insane—but awesome. Now it was a crazy reality with which he was professionally and emotionally involved. An intense friendship had formed among us in that short time. Still less than a mile away, we had almost disappeared—moving surprisingly fast for a fat rowboat.

Next to him was photographer Erinn Hale. She braced her arm on the side of the boat for one last shot. The water had already changed from the turbid brown of the Hudson estuary to the gray-green of the sea. Almost a year ago Erinn had sat next to Greg on a plane. He and Brad were returning from scouting out our departure point, and he told her about the race. For the price of tickets to New York and England, Erinn joined our team. She was banking on the idea that she could sell what photos she took of the ocean adventure. Like the row itself, her plan was a huge leap of faith. The skiff powered through the waves toward New York. Todd and Erinn were our last two friends to say good-bye. If everything went as planned, they would be the first to say hello on the other side of the sea.

—∿∿—

Dylan and Greg rowed with gusto. Only the red hull of the *Yorkshire Warrior* remained visible in the distance off Coney Island. A line of freighters queued up like massive apparitions in the distance ready to enter the Narrows. The west wind blew strong; it was impossible to turn around. We had won the unofficial six-mile race to the bridge, and now it was time to row the ocean—just 3194 miles to go.

Playing chicken with a freighter at the start of the race (Erinn J. Hale)

—◠◠◠—

Chapter 2

Inauspicious Starts

I swung the sledgehammer, knocking the new beam into place. Two wood four-by-fours jacked up the ceiling on either side, temporarily holding up the top of my house. It was 452 days before the race, and team headquarters would not be ready by the time the guys moved in. Flipping a house seemed like a feasible enterprise at the time. Lack of skill or life experiences had not kept me from purchasing a sketchy adjustable rate mortgage or deciding to row across the ocean. Adding the remodel seemed par for the course.

I had it all worked out. Dylan, Greg, Brad, and another of Chief Red Beard's rowers from UPS, Nick Edwards, would move into the house, and for discounted rent all would suffer through some minor construction. Dry dock in the backyard, office in the basement, barracks, and mess hall, all in one. I felt that bunking together was the best way to not just survive but win this race. Life among the plastic sheeting and the exposed wiring did not translate directly into ocean rowing, but there was a certain similar misery to it.

—◠◠◠—

Five months later the ridged steel doors of the rust-colored forty-foot container swung open. Warm air spilled out, enveloping the four of us at the warehouse. Fluorescent light revealed an unadorned primer-gray hull sitting on a trailer. We stood in awe of our purchase.

"Looks like it's not a scam," said Brad. Wiring just under forty thousand dollars from Seattle to a random bank account almost five thousand miles away in England took no small amount of trust. Especially considering the only confirmation we had of the company's existence was a website, a few phone calls, and some emails. But this was a very real boat. Whether our money had been well spent was yet to be decided. Regardless, with just under three hundred days before the race, we were now the proud owners of the seventh hull created from the Woodvale Ocean Fours boat mold.

It looked like the love child of a long ship and a V2 rocket. Built in Devon, England, of fiberglass and Kevlar, the eight-hundred-pound, twenty-nine-foot hull was built specifically for our North Atlantic race by the race organizer, Woodvale-Events (Woodvale), to have the best self-righting capabilities of any ocean rowboat yet built. It made its first Atlantic crossing by freighter to Canada, then by rail across the Great North. At the port of Vancouver, British Columbia, the boat sat anonymously among thousands of other steel boxes of commerce for three weeks. Painfully we waited for a railroad worker strike to end so our new toy could make the final 125-mile trip south across the border.

After attaching the trailer tongue to Greg's truck, I pulled myself awkwardly onto the deck, which seemed oddly expansive without equipment. Except for three hatches and four cleats, the gray hull and bulkheads were bare. Entering the tiny cabin—eight by five feet at its widest point and tapering to eighteen inches in the stern, or back end—required contorting my six-foot-five frame through a hatch barely wider than my shoulders. The gel-coated fiberglass was bright white. Imagining the four of us down here in a storm was unpleasant.

Each team would outfit their boat as they saw fit. Oars, seat, and rigger designs were entirely up to us. Our equipment would be designed to address every problem we had read about ocean rowing. Woodvale's packet of required gear and medicine did not include measurements about where the internal bulkheads were located within the craft. Cutting and fitting hatches and equipment would be made more difficult, as we had to guess each bulkhead's location beneath the deck.

Standing up from a clumsy exit out of the hatch, I tapped the bulkhead with my boots. "It's going to be a suffer fest," I assessed.

—⁓—

The craft sat in the backyard. It had not moved in several weeks. An inch-by-inch examination revealed damage to our brand-new forty-thousand-dollar boat. We sent pictures to Woodvale and waited for explanations and suggestions on how to mitigate the defects. Until we resolved the issue, we weren't eager to throw ourselves into outfitting the boat, so it sat as summer turned to fall. We waited a bit longer for a response from Woodvale and then looked elsewhere for advice. Eight months to go before we would row out of New York.

—⁓—

"Those are minor cracks, but definitely cracks." Jeff Knakal examined the bottom of the hull around the daggerboard housing. Jeff was part of Sound Rowers, a community of open-water rowers and paddlers in and around Seattle. A Boeing engineer, he fixed the occasional rowing shell on the side. Our hull had been built using a technique called sandwich construction. Several layers of fiberglass and Kevlar lay like bread slices over both sides of a foam core to create a lightweight, strong composite material.

"The danger is water getting into the foam between the fiberglass," Jeff explained. "Once it's in there, it will expand and contract with the temperature and will eventually degrade the hull—it should definitely be fixed." Greg and Dylan examined the cracks. Dylan stuck his fingernail in one. "It shouldn't be hard," said Jeff. "I'd be happy to help."

Our rowing coach, Bill Tytus, also expressed "great concern" over the cracks. He told us to keep the hull out of the water until it was fixed. We sent more pictures to Woodvale outlining the damage and queried other owners of the same type of craft. Greg learned that their boats saw similar problems. Two weeks later Woodvale ordered a survey of the boats. Teresa, our main contact there, assured us that the cracks were superficial and would "not affect the internal and/or external structural integrity of the boat in any way." We respectfully sought out second opinions.

A week later, the marine surveyor's report confirmed what Woodvale stated as technically true but added: "If left untreated, there is the potential for water ingress and, ultimately, structural degradation." Woodvale had built a strong boat. However, unsealed plywood was built into the daggerboard housing and already had soaked up some water while sitting on its trailer in rainy England. It had expanded and contracted in the heat and begun to crack where the daggerboard was inserted. It was not yet a problem, but unaddressed, water would continue to work its way into the laminated foam and fiberglass, eventually detaching the two and degrading the foam.

It would be an expensive and difficult repair. Considering the money already invested, we didn't want to pay the two thousand extra dollars quoted by various boat shops to get our boat up to snuff. If we did have to pay, we wanted some equivalent reductions in the race fee.

The cracks were not our only concern. The rudder and the removable daggerboard that stood in for a keel on the small boat looked to Jeff and other experienced boatmen to be of questionable integrity. It did not take a sailor's eye to tell something was up: the daggerboard itself did not fit into its cracked housing. We managed to get it in just over a quarter of the way before it held so fast we thought it might be stuck for good. Nor was it straight.

Our suspicions were confirmed when many of the men who would become our mentors reacted with either grave concern or outright laughter. One of these was Robert H. Perry. When Bob double-parked his silver Mercedes next to our still primer-gray boat parked on the street, we were not sure what to think of him. He had salt-and-pepper hair and a Scottish Black Watch cap on. To our pleasant surprise, we found that Bob knew a little something about offshore sailboats. Considered the father of performance cruising sailboat design, more than five thousand boats of his design cut wakes across the world's oceans. Bob and his two assistants, Ben and Tristan, happened to work less than a mile from our house.

Sizing up our rudder and daggerboard carefully, Bob pronounced them, in his professional opinion, "pieces of shit." He offered to write Woodvale to tell them so, this time referring to the appendages as "crudely built and in need of immediate rebuilding." In his letter, he listed nine major issues with them, alleviating any lingering doubt we had that our concerns were well founded.

In her valiantly polite style, long-suffering Teresa wrote back: "This is a yacht designer/manufacturer putting tolerances on items that simply don't compare." She went on to say that the "crude" speeds of our rowboat "would not highlight any noticeable difference in performance with these imperfections in fairing, foil shape, or symmetry." While her assertion that an increase in speed equals an increase in drag was true, Teresa would not be the one dragging a rowboat thirty-two hundred miles to England. Bob looked at it from the perspective that it was still a twenty-nine-foot boat going across one of the world's roughest stretches of water. Even if we were willing to tolerate all those imperfections, the daggerboard would still be impossible to use since it could not fit into the housing.

So Bob Perry and his crew designed two daggerboards and one rudder for us. The original rudder was not bent and thus salvageable, so we had it reinforced with carbon. We would go to sea with at least one spare for each major piece of equipment. Anything less felt irresponsible.

The plain, unmodified boat, before going into drydock in our backyard

—◠◠—

Chapter 3

Risky Business

"Do you know what it's like to be denied for a loan three times in a row?" Dylan's voice trembled. We sat in the basement office at HQ next to Nick's bedroom, whose door was open. The carpet was stained and the wood-paneled walls had an aged purple hue. Two weak lights augmented the late fall daylight let in by one tiny window. Three desks were pushed up against the walls covered with maps and boating posters. A huge to-do list was pinned on an easel.

We had agreed that each crewmate was responsible for putting up an equal and significant chunk of cash to get the project off the ground, showing potential sponsors that we were not asking for their money without assuming the same risk. All agreed this was essential. But $12,500 was a lot of money—the price of a car, a semester at a private college, or a couple of years at a public school—and Dylan could not come up with it. With just over eight months before our launch date, hard decisions had to be made. Greg's parents could afford to give him a loan. Brad took bonds his parents had saved for him since childhood. And my story was complicated.

—◠◠—

When I was three years old, my father died unexpectedly. The sting of his sudden death and the success of a century-old family business were inseparably intertwined with my sense of financial freedom. I had been able to go to the college I wanted. I had been able to invest in a house at twenty-one. I am the son of a fourth-generation scale manufacturer. Hanson Scale Company made products that weighed everything from babies to bales of cotton. Started in Chicago in 1888 by my great-great-grandfather Marius Hansen, the business eventually moved to Ireland, England, France, and finally to New Mexico. Four generations of sons headed the factory—my father, Jim Hanssen, was the last to join the business shortly after he married my mother, Eve.*

My father was in his early thirties when he was left in charge of the factory in Europe. His younger brother, my Uncle Eric, had joined my grandparents in New Mexico. Early in the morning on August 15, 1985, eleven days after my third birthday and fewer than eighteen months after moving my mother and me from Ireland to England, my father collapsed in the hallway outside my room. It was an asthma attack. We saw his impossible struggle to take a breath. He was drowning on land and we could not help him. He died in front of us.

When the storm of grief blew over, we landed in the small town of Las Cruces, New Mexico, surrounded by family. I grew up visiting the factory, familiar with the tang of machine oil and the thunder of steel presses. My cousins and I played among the silent machines as the adults worked weekends. Secretaries referred to me as "young Mr. Hanssen," a subtly feigned deference that was lost on me. Everyone took orders from Grandpa Stan, Uncle Hugo, and especially 250-pound, six-foot-nine Uncle Eric, whom I realized—even at three—was an enormous adult. As a child I assumed that I would one day work at the factory, but I was fifteen when the business was sold and my inheritance set.

———

I sat with my crewmates in the HQ basement, arguing over money—or the lack of it. We needed money if we were going to move forward. The first three investments had come to $37,500. Greg had paid $2,700 on top of this as a 10-percent down payment for Woodvale

---

* You have probably noticed three separate spellings of the family name. "Hansen" is the name Marius carried over with him from Denmark. A Chicago mailman suggested changing the company name to "Hanson" because it would sound more "American." And the family name changed when Marius's son, my great-grandfather Stanly Hansen, had the same bank as a man of the same name. To keep accounts separate, he changed his name to Stan Lee Hanssen, and we have kept that spelling ever since.

to start building the hull, and I had put in another $2,200 to make a race payment. This got us the boat, its trailer, shipment from Europe, and the first monthly payments we had to make toward the total race fee. We were spending money faster than we could raise it. Our war chest had shrunk to less than five hundred dollars, and the boat still had wooden prototype equipment. We needed Dylan's share if we were going to actually outfit this boat, but he could not get a bank loan.

"What if I can't raise it?" he asked. "There is no one, absolutely no one, I can ask."

The three of us were silent. I stared uncomfortably at the floor. Each of my crewmates had, by proportion, risked far more than I. What could we expect from Dylan? He had invested ten months of his life, conscious it might come to this moment. He had kept up scholarships, worked through college, and was about to sell his car to make it through the next few months. Labor, mental or physical, was not an esoteric concept for him. I thought I could work hard— Dylan *knew* he could.

I struggled through the possible outcomes. Would we cast him aside for someone with cash? Having three of the four take the financial risk did not seem fair. We would have absolutely nothing to show for our investment if we did not row the ocean. Right now Dylan had *time* invested, but what if he came to the realization that rowing across the ocean was bat-shit crazy, and he walked?

"What if we take what you guys invested and divided it by four?" he asked. It would not solve the current problem of not having any money. "If we don't raise the money, then I will pay you guys my share. It might take some time, but if we make it to New York or not, I will sign a contract saying so."

Dylan had bared his neck. If we had assumed for the past ten months that we would row across the ocean with him, we must have trusted each other. His commitment was made if we were willing to accept it. I looked at Brad and Greg. Greg was visibly uncomfortable with this situation; I did not know what he would say if he spoke first. Brad would almost certainly side with Dylan if it came down to it, but his silence was difficult to read. I could feel the fabric of our team starting to tear and I filled the silence.

"Dylan, you don't have to sign a thing."

The crew and Nick toast after receiving over fifteen thousand dollars in grants for our organizations.

—⌒⌒—

Chapter 4

Goddamn Geniuses

Greg was ready to quit after the meeting. Seven months until race day, and the project had become a pain in the ass—a lot of work and very little rowing. Two practices a day had slipped to every other day, and his conditioning was evaporating. He lived in a construction site. He was uncomfortable with Dylan's lack of investment. Most of all, he hated living with Brad. Despite having had the same rowing coach at the same school, they had never rowed together and seemed to have little in common. Something about Brad had begun irritating him—he never appeared to do any work, never asked for help, yet he consistently produced great results overnight, seemingly out of nowhere. Greg worried it was going to get the team into trouble.

Why the hell am I doing this? Greg wondered. He'd wanted to quit a few months back too, so why hadn't he? Seeing the boat in person, cracks and all, had made the idea real. Greg had decided to wait and see how the meeting at the Seattle Yacht Club Foundation went. We were hoping for grant money from them to support the adventure. Then he would make his decision about moving forward.

At the time, though, the rest of us had no idea that Greg was waffling. With the constant ring of phone calls and the flurry of emails coming from him, no one thought of him quitting. Greg deserved credit for his dedication. I doubted I would have agreed to such an outlandish proposal—hey guys, let's traverse the Atlantic Ocean in a rowboat!—had someone else proposed it, especially if he were four or five years younger than me.

I was the link between them all, old enough to have interacted a little with Greg while in college and young enough to have developed a strong rapport with Dylan and Brad. I assumed this was why I was voted captain—that and the fact I had been the primary instigator. If Greg had shown interest in being captain, I would have bowed to his seniority. He never asked.

—◇◇◇—

Later that afternoon I found Nick working in his dungeonlike room next to our basement office. He had overheard the entire money conversation. I had been pacing the house, hoping to God we could keep it together. Wiping the tears from my eyes, I looked at Nick and laughed. "For someone getting ready to do something really tough, I seem to be crying a lot."

Nick looked at me thoughtfully. "It's because this is the toughest you've ever been." Advice and motivational quips like this were a natural benefit of having the editor-in-chief of *The Internationalist* magazine as a friend and housemate. Nick, one of my best friends, had decided to quit rowing his senior year to start a quarterly nonpartisan foreign-policy magazine. Only after I saw his passion with the magazine could I forgive him for not rowing. The organized chaos of Nick, four other principals, and thirty unpaid interns churning out the award-winning quarterly blew me away. *The Internationalist* ran on an idea and passion. This inspired me, providing fertile ground for my own crazy idea to grow.

—◇◇◇—

That had all been a year ago. Since then OAR Northwest and *The Internationalist* had shared a parallel course guided by blind faith and ego, inspiring both organizations to walk the line between success and failure on a daily basis. OAR Northwest had just met with the Seattle Yacht Club Foundation. The day had been equally big for *The Internationalist*. I called Nick. "How was the day?" I asked cautiously.

"It went well. How was yours?" he asked, just as carefully.

The energy of the five of us in the house created a buzz that almost—but not quite—made up for the decision to keep the heat off that winter to save money. Tonight made up for the cold.

"We won today."

"So did we," he said.

———〜〜———

A half hour later the five of us convened in the kitchen. We clinked unmatched glasses from crystal flutes to canning jars with five-dollar champagne. On the same day, months of navigating the labyrinth of grants and sponsorships had finally resulted in victory for us both—a seven-thousand-dollar grant for *The Internationalist* and an eight-thousand-dollar grant for OAR Northwest from the Seattle Yacht Club Foundation. More than two thousand additional dollars had come from individual donations from yacht club members. Apparently, the five of us at team HQ were no longer the only ones who believed in each other. Fewer than seven months remained, and tonight we were invincible.

A plastic Tyrannosaurus rex looked over us from his usual perch on the shelf above the stove. Rex had become our unofficial mascot. I poked the button on his thigh. The terrible little lizard king waved his tiny arms and roared his approval.

———〜〜———

Larry Schildwachter surveyed the boat outside the Emerald Harbor Marine office at Elliott Bay Marina. "What the hell is with this chintzy wooden rigging?" He looked hard and a bit puzzled at it, as if he were thinking, *Not a single one of these guys has had a night of deep-water experience, and they expect to row this gray phallus across the ocean?*

"What is this stuff?" he asked Dylan, gesturing with visible skepticism toward the seats. Dylan explained they were simply prototypes to make sure we got the seat height right. Larry didn't want to help us, but we were like puppies. *These guys certainly have an abundance of optimism,* he remembers thinking. "Don't worry," he sighed. "We'll get you guys sorted out." He bid us goodbye, turning back into his office. Just out of earshot, he leaned over and whispered to his friend Dan Heyl: "If we don't help these guys, they're going to fucking die."

I liked to think of Larry as our hard-ass with the heart of gold. Combined, he and Dan had tens of thousands of miles of racing and offshore sailing experience. Their task was to make this vessel trustworthy. Larry surrounded himself with competent people, and he steered us toward some of the best boating hands in Seattle. Each phone number and introduction was followed with "He's the best" or "The guy's a goddamn genius."

I once asked Larry how one man could know so many goddamn geniuses.

"I figured a good way to run a business is to surround myself with people smarter than me," he explained.

Larry gave us a key to use the Emerald Harbor shop, much to the dismay of the Emerald Harbor crew, who were often, understandably, frustrated by four inexperienced kids taking up their space. As the hours in the shop began to add up and the boat took shape, their initial annoyance turned into grudging respect and, later, enthusiasm. (This of course was augmented by the cases of beer we left in the shop before we headed for New York.)

———

Six months before the race, on New Year's Eve, my girlfriend Rebecca, and I worked on prototype oar blades in the backyard late into the evening. It was one of dozens of jobs to complete before the big Seattle Boat Show a month away. Unlike me, Rebecca had actually spent some of her adult life working at a boat shop. We had met eight months earlier. I'd been her coach at an adult evening rowing league at the Lake Washington Rowing Club, where I trained. I had some reservations dating someone I was coaching, but the fact she was two years my senior balanced this out. As midnight approached, we walked into the street to watch the fireworks over the Space Needle. We held hands and said "I love you" for the first time.

———

"That is a crazy idea," I said.

Greg shook his head in disbelief. "No, we're rowing across the ocean—*that* is a crazy idea."

We were looking for a publicity stunt of some kind to demonstrate to the boat show vendors and potential sponsors that we were serious. Greg proposed that we keep a rowing machine moving for the entire duration of the show, day and night. I felt that this miserable device distills out all the intrinsic pleasure of the sport, much as a treadmill does for running. The longest I had ever rowed on one of these machines was an hour and a half. According to Greg's plan, each man would have two three-hour shifts over a twenty-four-hour period, covering roughly twenty-three miles a shift. In nine days we would clock enough miles to cover the distance from Seattle to Chicago. We would sleep and shower in the locker rooms at the event center. How well it would work attracting sponsors was hard to say, but the physical conditioning would certainly do us good. Sadly, that aspect was becoming less of a priority as the search for sponsorship and working on the boat intensified. We would be grateful for the pain.

—◊—

Several days into the boat show I had grown accustomed to the sweat-soaked boredom of the rowing machine on a platform above the crowd. At night we watched movies as the security guards periodically checked in on us. During the day, the lone rower people-watched, leaving the talking to a crewmate, while the other two napped, ate, or stayed up to help if they had the energy. On one particular shift I noticed Dylan and Brad talking with a sturdy-looking man of medium height with a brown mustache. He mimed a shape on top of our wooden prototype rigging that looked something like a rail. They nodded vigorously, but I couldn't hear their exchange. The man was Dave Robertson, owner of Gig Harbor Boat Works. For almost twenty years he had been building classic rowing boats from sturdy fiberglass trimmed with wood, with a unique sliding seat. Dave had built the best ocean-rowing sliding seat in existence and didn't know it until he saw our boat.

A pervasive annoyance, common to many rowboats, is the noise made by the sliding seat. Flat-water racing shells have sliding seats, while most fishing dories and dinghies generally do not. A sliding seat allows the oarsmen to take advantage of considerable leg power, an advantage we would not go to sea without. In an ocean-rowing environment, with the destructive characteristics of salt water, the typical sliding seat system is apt to need replacing or servicing throughout the voyage. Blogs and notes from other ocean rowers cited both frequent breakdown and the obnoxious sound as among the more horrible experiences of the endeavor. We detested the thought of hearing that noise for months, twenty-four hours a day. It was a problem we wanted to solve.

Dave had wanted his rowboats to have the advantage of a sliding seat. Dissatisfied with what existed, he built his own out of fiberglass, stainless steel, and eight Rollerblade wheels. Each boat had a pair of fiberglass channels, about as wide as the wheel, topped with a piece of aluminum. Four of these wheels were installed vertically on the seat so they would slide into the channel and provide a smooth, silent slide for the rower. The other four wheels were added horizontally to the bottom, blocking it from jamming from side to side. Dave Robertson had set out to create a seat that would need little if any maintenance over its lifetime, and it was also completely silent. After seeing our boat and learning of our intended expedition, Dave knew he could create exactly what we'd been looking for.

—∕∕∕—

Because of our distance from England, Woodvale Events, the race organizer, allowed us to put together a navigational course of our own in lieu of the required Royal Yacht Club courses. Our navigator of choice, David Burch, had a not-so-secret lair—Starpath School of Navigation—in Ballard, Seattle's old Scandinavian quarter. Boxes and stacks of navigation books for sale were piled up warehouse-style next to the front door. A shelf spanning an entire far wall was filled with more. Several folding tables lined the opposite wall and filled up the middle of the large open room. On them were stacked computers, charts, bits and pieces of the latest course-plotting electronics, several sextants, pre-internet navigational paraphernalia stretching back hundreds of years, and several types of global positioning system (GPS) receivers. The worldwide system of GPS satellites that triangulate positions through small handheld devices has augmented the important compass for navigation. Scattered about in between was an equally diverse array of workout equipment. Above the tables was a cardboard sign reading: "Please excuse our mess. We are scheduled for completion in 2015." On the narrow strip of wall between the floor-to-ceiling windows was an old map labeled "Falmouth Harbor"—our intended destination across the Atlantic. It was a good omen.

David Burch was of average height and solidly built, with a neatly trimmed white beard that made his age hard to place. When Greg and I first ventured to the navigation school, he had been busy and totally unimpressed with our mission. After hearing us out with a polite expression on his face, Burch smiled and asked, "What neighborhood do you live in?"

Greg and I exchanged confused glances. "Wallingford," I offered.

"If you're going to row across the ocean, you should probably live in Ballard," said David wistfully. It was a nod to Ballard's Scandinavian roots and specifically to George Harbo and Frank Samuelsen, the two Norwegian supermen who first rowed the North Atlantic in 1896. How living two whole neighborhoods away would affect our success, I was not sure. However, Burch seemed like a really smart guy. He agreed to teach the navigation class. Before we left that night, he gave us what he considered a light two-hour course overview.

Over the next few months of classes, Dylan and Greg excelled and seemingly "got" navigation. Brad and I were mediocre-to-poor students. David was only slightly aware of the late nights we spent working on the boat. As we approached race day, he realized, *Christ, they are actually going to do this!* Like Larry and Dan before him, Burch possessed knowledge that we—aspiring to become men of the sea—could not possibly know. Fortunately, he decided to help us, gratis.

—⁓—

Oars communicate human exertion to the water, so we regarded any improvement to them as worthwhile. The last half of the twentieth century saw two major developments in the technology: the material and the shape. In the late 1970s fiberglass, and eventually carbon fiber, replaced wooden shafts and blades. Flat-water racing oars are made today exclusively of these lighter, stronger materials. Blade shape was another innovation. The older flat-water racing blades were long, symmetrical, and skinny—very similar to oars built for rowing workboats. In the 1960s these oar blades were replaced by a wider symmetrical blade known as a "Macon" that placed more surface area below the water. In the 1990s an asymmetrical blade was created. The design put even more surface area below the water. In flat-water race boats, rowing in calm conditions, the hatchet-shaped blade has become the ubiquitous competitive blade of choice.

After extensive research, we concluded that most, if not all, modern ocean-rowing equipment was merely a built-up or adjusted version of flat-water gear. The only equipment specifically designed for ocean rowing was the hull itself. The result was that teams brought up to eight oars on a row, expecting half to break. No one appeared to have taken into account that all this equipment had been highly specialized over the past 150 years for the singular purpose of rowing small, fragile boats on calm, freshwater.

For advice on oars (and most everything about rowing), we only had to go as far as the Lake Washington Rowing Club, about a mile from my house, where Frank Cunningham and Bill Tytus coached. Bill was the third man to run Pocock Racing Shells, a company that had built rowing shells for almost a hundred years. Frank was remarkably spry for eighty-four. He had been rowing since fourteen and claimed to have taken only one perfect stroke— at the age of seventy. It was a story he liked to tell to keep the confidence of his rowers in check. Frank had been coached by men who had professionally raced rowboats back when rowing was one of the most popular (and heavily bet on) sports in North America. Once a professional sport with working-class roots and a huge popular following, gambling led to its downfall around the turn of the century. Eventually the public had its limit of races thrown or rigged, and the sport fell out of favor. Rowing has continued to exist on an amateur level at elite high schools, colleges, and private clubs, where it got its reputation as an upper-class sport.

The combined experience of Bill and Frank spans more than a century of rowing, fixing, and building boats, as well as coaching at every level. Their suggestion to use wooden oars with symmetrical blades surprised us. "I can beat a wood oar with a hammer all day long and it's going to dent, and you can still row with it," Bill explained. "Carbon will fracture." Thus I learned that "strength" and "toughness" are different qualities. Carbon oars may be stronger than wood, but they are not as tough. In the middle of nowhere—the ocean, for example—durability remains king. Bill and Frank also reminded us that the famed Norwegians Harbo and Samuelsen had used wooden oars over a hundred years ago, and their fifty-five-day record for crossing the Atlantic still stood. The virtue of using symmetrical blades was more obvious to us. They can be rowed on both sides of the boat with equal efficiency, meaning that we could bring fewer spares and therefore less clutter. The long, skinny blade shape was far more versatile than the hatchet in a variety of water conditions. This was important because we decided that we would not feather the oars—that is, turn the blade horizontal to the water to gain clearance as we reached for the next stroke. This motion, which is critical to flat-water rowing, seemed like something we could omit, considering the geometry of our robust craft.

—⁓—

Frank and Bill's advice on oars, combined with an introduction through Dave Robertson, led us to Bruce Bergstrom. He ran a paddle and oar factory amid small hills of sawdust and wood chips in the town of Talent, along Oregon's Interstate 5 corridor. Bruce had a big beard and a sinewy frame from a lifetime of paddling and woodworking. In short, he looked like a wooden oar maker. Inside his factory, men covered in bits of ash and pine wrangled well-oiled World War II–era woodworking machines to produce oars and paddles on an industrial scale with a craftsman's touch.

Greg and I calculated the measurements for our oars using a mix of geometry and guesswork. An oar works with the rigger like a lever and fulcrum. Where the fulcrum is placed will determine the amount of mechanical advantage. The shaft of the oar has two sections. The inboard comes up from the rigger and into the handle; the outboard extends out the other side of the rigger to the blade, into the water. The shorter the ratio of the inboard to the outboard section, the higher the load. Conversely, the longer the inboard section is compared to the outboard, the lighter the load. Gearing a lighter load reduced the risk of injury. Installing outriggers gave us an extra foot of total inboard space to work with, allowing us to increase the load and keep the same gearing.

After scrutinizing our calculations for over an hour, Bruce suggested ash for its great durability, resilience, and excellent strength-to-weight ratio. He custom-built the handles to be larger than average, fashioning several grips to work against fatigue. The oar shafts would be wrapped in a carbon-fiber sleeve for added strength and stiffness, allowing the diameter of the shaft to be smaller and lighter. The only drawback was that this carbon-fiber sleeve was the same material that turned the oars into lightning rods. Bruce did not have enough time to craft the blades, so I turned to a popular flat-water oar maker, Concept2. They agreed to cut them out of their existing large Macon mold to create a long, skinny, symmetrical blade close to the one I imagined.

Our oars came together two nights before our first major training cruise. In the backyard under hot halogen lamps steaming in the cold late-winter air, the two-part epoxy we'd mixed smelled powerfully of rotten eggs. We slid each black carbon-covered shaft into the receiving end of the blade and let it set. After the addition of white paint, a logo, and a nylon tether for extra precaution, the oars weighed in at a stout ten pounds each. This was twice the weight of flat-water oars of the same length, but we would only take two spares, half the usual redundancy. The gross weight of our six oars outweighed eight average oars by ten pounds, but durability was worth it.

Chapter 5

—⟋⋁⋁⟍—

Sponsorship, Training, and Countdown

The journey is the thing.
—Homer

The decision to raise money for the American Lung Association of Washington (ALAW) transformed the spirit of my father from a quiet specter in my past to a daily presence. The race manual had suggested partnering with a cause: We would provide a story, and the charity would get publicity. The association with a respected charity would give us credibility, contacts, and recognition.

The most valuable asset a charity had for us, however, was the 501(c)(3) not-for-profit classification. So armed, an organization becomes endowed with the following powers: it is not taxed by the Internal Revenue Service, and all donations are tax deductible for donors, often the deciding factor for whether or not people will give. The challenge was meeting the IRS's criteria, which would take many months. We had more than one ten-thousand-dollar donation waiting to be made contingent upon our securing the not-for-profit status. It surprised us, though, to find out just how many people were willing to give solely based on the challenge of rowing the ocean, tax-deductible or no. Until receiving the classification, we functioned under the umbrella of the charity organization that we convinced to partner with us.

We had approached ALAW about three months into our preparation. ALAW was the ideal organization to partner with based on the simple fact that rowing uses lungs and ALAW cares about them. It was a positive association but didn't really hold a candle

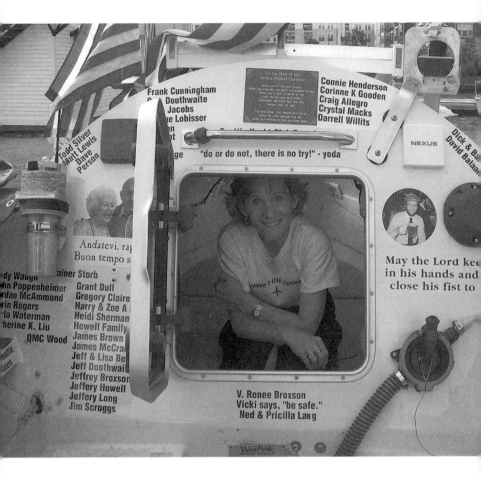

My mother, Eve, sits in the cabin next to the picture of my father she and my stepfather, Jim Wood, put on the boat.

to the compelling human-interest story of a young boy watching his father die from asthma after living with it his whole life. Raising money is hard, relentless work; adding an emotional component to fund-raising reminds people why they give. My sad and easy-to-relate-to story was a perfect one to raise money with.

ALAW is housed in a nondescript building in Seattle, located behind a bus stop filled with chain-smokers. Our initial meeting was the first time I had told my story in such detail in front of people I did not know. I'd compartmentalized my father's death since I was three, developing a concise account of what happened so I could swiftly move any conversation along after thanking someone for his or her sympathy. I focused on the effort to keep my composure. ALAW agreed to partner with us. With the thrill of victory, though, came a feeling that I was feeding off my father's corpse. But if we could put their sticker on our boat and raise some money and awareness along the way, then a part of me supposed that the end result outweighed my guilt. I wondered how my family, and my father, would feel about sharing his death with so many people.

Over the next few weeks, Brad, Dylan, and Greg each came to me individually with the suggestion that we should name the boat after my dad. I had wanted this but did not feel I could ask that of my teammates, since it would limit sponsorship options, and sponsorship sells visibility. Our team name as well as the name of our rowboat were all up for grabs—for a price. All we had to sell besides a good feeling was a bit of real estate on the side of a rowboat in an obscure race in an obscure sport with the flimsy guarantee that what we were trying to do was so off the wall that it might get national attention. Asking to limit anything we could sell did not seem like the best decision with forty thousand dollars sunk into the project. In spite of this, my teammates made it clear that we honor my father first.

After the boat was christened—the *James Robert Hanssen*— people who had known my father had a reason to say his name again. People who did not know him said it too. For the first time in my life, I heard his name spoken with tones of hope instead of nostalgia and sadness. This simple act transformed that cold, inanimate hull and gave me back, in a small but measurable way, some of my father. The boys had willfully, if not intentionally, allowed the expedition to be steered into a meaning beyond the physical for me.

Cold water poured over the gunwale (the topside edge) of the steel
lifeboat. Rain belted us like a fire hose, and on the small deck we
struggled to unpack our survival suits. We unrolled them, frantically
pulling on the ridiculous-looking orange neoprene survival costumes
appropriately nicknamed "Gumby suits." Now, seventy-five days
before go time, the four of us were enduring a week of training at
the Seattle Maritime Academy docks, under the shadow of the Ballard Bridge.

Greg, Dylan, and I zipped our suits as water reached our thighs.
They dove toward the white fiberglass keg containing the life raft. I
swam for Angela Madsen, our "injured" crewmate, to assist her into
the life raft. Angela had joined us for the training to get ready for
her own ocean row. A paraplegic ex-Marine, she had taught herself
to walk with the use of leg braces. She has won several gold medals
rowing in the Paralympics.

I looked for Brad, hoping to get help, but he moved sluggishly.
Water had filled his survival suit, and it was all he could do to get to
the life raft. Greg manually triggered the inflation device. There was
a crack and hiss as the built-in CO_2 canister released. In seconds,
the raft unfolded into a flimsy structure the size and shape of a
two-man tent with a tiny entrance portal. Men and women in scuba
gear tugged at us, imitating the separating power of wave action.
Dylan and Greg clambered through the opening and reached out to
pull Angela up as I lifted her from behind. The water in Brad's suit
doubled his weight as we hauled him into the raft. I was the last one
pulled into the cramped florescent-orange six-person life raft.

The rain felt like a fire hose because it was a fire hose. This was
a drill, and we passed, but the exhausted faces around me mirrored
concern. Would this performance be enough to survive on the open
ocean?

—∿∿—

It was two months before the race and we were on our first training
cruise in the Puget Sound when our daggerboard broke. Construction of our new daggerboards and rudder was not ready in time
for this cruise that had brought us to the west side of San Juan
Island. Knowing we might need the board anyway, we had sanded
the thicker areas of the daggerboard to make it fit. To Woodvale's

credit, our decision to do this may have weakened the daggerboard from its original construction, but this would not excuse the bent, asymmetrical construction that had warranted sanding it in the first place.

"Jordan, kick the steering over. We're getting too close," said Dylan, a third time. It was taking me a while to learn how to steer properly. This time my ineptitude was not the problem. The wind blew firmly from the west, producing a moderate two- to three-foot chop blowing us into San Juan Island.

"It's kicked over as far as it will go," I said.

"We shouldn't be getting this close to land," Dylan said. Dylan was rarely this short with anyone.

"It's all the way over," I insisted.

Greg stepped outside the cabin as the exchange heated up. He wore his favorite red-and-beige-striped wool cap with earflap ties that looked like braided, blond hair. "What's going on, boys?" he asked while chewing a large candy bar.

"The boat keeps moving toward shore," I said. "I've got the rudder kicked over as far as it will go."

Greg gestured nonchalantly with his candy bar to the side of the boat closest to land. The boat acted as a windbreak, creating a small patch of calm water called a wind shadow. "That's probably why," he said.

I looked over to see the bottom half of our daggerboard floating next to the hull, apparently where it had been for as long as Dylan and I had noticed our drift. Surprised, I yanked it to safety. Although shocked at the loss and its implications, I was amazed to see the exposed jagged cross section of pale yellow foam and thin fiberglass. Even with my novice eye, it appeared too lightly built.

"Hey Brad, the daggerboard broke," Dylan called. Brad crawled out on deck and the four of us stared blankly at each other.

"What are our options?" I asked.

"We should put out the sea anchor," said Greg.

Dylan suggested we call the Coast Guard and let them know our situation. We all looked at each other, waiting for someone to give the order.

After a moment I stepped in. "Brad, you and Greg set the sea anchor. Dylan and I will call the Coast Guard and work on a fix." I got on the VHF (very high frequency) radio and turned to emergency channel 16. Dylan pulled out the yellow logbook and recorded our situation.

I reached the Coast Guard and in my most amiable and nonpanicked voice I explained the deal: "We're in a rowboat... an ocean rowboat... it's a big rowboat.... Yes, built specifically for crossing oceans.... Yes, sir, we have life vests, lifelines too.... No, sir, we don't need a tow." From his routine monotone, it sounded like a boring day at the office. "We are currently performing a repair... Yes, that is correct, a twenty-nine-foot red-and-white ocean rowboat.... No, no sails.... No engine either, just oars.... Thank you. Will call you in a half hour with an update."

Greg and Brad struggled on deck. The upper half of the daggerboard was stuck fast in its housing. Wrapping rope around the exposed lip of the board, they began heaving precariously. The waves turned the boat uncomfortably on its beam. Dylan and I began to brainstorm, nausea overwhelming me. If we could not row away from shore in this wind without a daggerboard, then besides getting a tow, there was only one option. We could take the longer bottom half that had been floating in the wind shadow, shove it into the housing, and hope it had sufficient surface area to give our rudder enough purchase to turn the boat. The daggerboard's loss proved its significance. The extra surface area below the waterline stabilized the boat in choppy waves and allowed the boat to take a greater angle into the wind, thereby increasing the boat's maneuverability in a variety of conditions.

Outside the cabin I heard cheers and jubilant swearing. The upper half of the old daggerboard blew in the wind on the end of the rope Brad and Greg had used to muscle it out. Dylan and I crudely duct-taped the jagged edges of the bottom half and drilled some holes into the board with a knife to put a rope handle through. I passed the stumpy board outside. Brad and Greg shoved it into place and began to row.

It worked. I called back the Coast Guard. "Our fix worked and we are back on course for Friday Harbor."

"What's your ETA?" asked the man on duty.

"About four or five hours."

"Why so long?"

"We are a rowboat," I explained, eliciting a giggle out of Dylan. As Greg would later write in the logbook, it was excellent practice in emergency management.

———

The hassle of dealing with cracks in our hull and the shoddy construction of the daggerboard was enough for us to limit our pre-race relations with Woodvale to the mandatory monthly payment. When the axle of the British-built boat trailer we had bought from Woodvale caught fire on I-5, we didn't bother mentioning it to them.

With two weeks to go before leaving for New York, Greg and I were driving back from an event at Gig Harbor Boat Works, about forty miles south of Seattle. Publicity for our expedition was gearing up and cars drove by, drivers waving in recognition. We returned the waves with gusto, feeling pretty self-important. One enthusiastic passerby motioned for us to roll down our window. "Your wheel's on fire!" he yelled.

We pulled off at the last possible median before the downtown Seattle exits. Ours was the last call for the tow truck driver that day. His huge flatbed truck was the only vehicle available after 5:00 PM capable of hauling both the boat and the trailer back to the shop.

With Woodvale's shoddy construction, and now this, we considered ourselves alone in this endeavor. Our mantra was "the safest crossing is the fastest crossing." We planned to show up and row, with or without Woodvale, and race whichever boats made it to the starting line.

———

I chuckled nervously as I lit what was essentially a flamethrower. Aiming the business end into the air, I gave it a few harmless test blasts, jetting flames four feet into the air. Greg and his father Dave stood back and admired their handiwork in wrapping the boat in sturdy heat-shrink plastic to cover up the bright red-and-white paint job and the kaleidoscope of sponsor stickers, great and small, that had got us to this point. According to Larry, the wrap would keep the boat clean and protected as it voyaged to the eastern seaboard on a flatbed. Now I turned the flamethrower toward the boat. With each wave of the flaming wand, the beige plastic sucked to the boat. I grew confident with each pass and began to enjoy it—very aware that if the boat combusted, it would be captured on Todd Soliday's high-def camera.

Three weeks before, Dylan had made several last-ditch cold calls to local film companies. In a remarkable stroke of luck, Flying Spot Entertainment decided our story was worth telling and outfitted us with the ability to film our trip. From that point on, they shadowed us until we were out of sight of land. After that, it was up to us to shoot the story with their equipment.

In-kind and cash donations, sponsorship, and our own money added up to roughly $150,000. With the documentary in full swing and over a year of work already invested, publicity had ramped up. Interviews with CNN, *20/20*, and *Good Morning America* were scheduled for the last week before the race. Too much was at stake for last-minute misadventure. "If one of us gets sick or injured," I told Nick, "I'm going to send you a ticket to New York. All you need is your passport." Like the rest of us, Nick had rowed for Chief Red Beard and loyalty ran deep. If OAR Northwest needed an extra body, he would catch the first flight out.

2 Days till Race

Although the race was billed as from New York to England, the boats were actually docked across from Manhattan in Jersey City, at the Liberty Landing Marina. All lined up next to each other in the unpaved boatyard, the crafts looked similar at first glance. But had our opponents come up with some critical idea that had escaped us? The *Seven Oaks* had a beefy steering system—not to mention a DVD player. The large lever could be manhandled for easy steering, but it required another man on deck—in addition to the rowers—to steer.

The *Commando Joe* had a massive stainless steel electronics platform screwed to the gunwale of the boat. Their communication electronics were a few inches higher and certainly more secure than ours, but cumbersome compared to our light plastic attachments.

The only bit of equipment we coveted was the *Yorkshire Warrior*'s flexible solar panels made of a material durable enough to walk on. One such panel was screwed to the front of our boat—the only one Larry Schildwachter happened to have lying around the Emerald

Harbor Marine office. Supply issues had made the more flexible panels unavailable to us. The solution had been to use a heavy, older—but reliable and efficient—stiff solar panel that required a big aluminum bracket to attach it to the curved outer bulkhead of the rear cabin. Harnessing sun power, we could charge two heavy marine batteries located in one of the central deck hatches to power a variety of equipment, including a water desalinization unit, a VHF radio, a satellite phone, a computer, a compass, and a GPS receiver. In case this sturdy system failed, we packed manual and alternate battery-powered backups of everything.

The competitions' sliding seats, raised and bolted to aluminum I beams, looked small on the comparatively large deck of the ocean rowboats. We knew they would become atrociously loud and sticky once at sea. In contrast, our boat had been outfitted with Dave Robertson's durable sliding seats. Our foot steering system, essentially a design from a flat-water boat built with durable sailboat hardware, meant that one person could both steer and row the boat, if it came to that. Nothing on any other boat made any one of us want to jump ship.

One area we felt well matched in was fitness—or our lack of it. We were certainly the tallest team. All the other rowers seemed to be built more like Dylan. Strangers walking through the marina would not see "athletes" but sixteen focused, fleshy men. We told the media our strategy was "rowing into shape," and we hoped it was true. In the six months leading up to the race, the extent of our physical training was those nine consecutive days on the rowing machine at the boat show, a seven-day cruise in Puget Sound, and a three-day row in the Pacific. Other than that, we worked sixteen-hour days and ate whatever we got our hands on. Our friends who knew us from training at the boathouse were worried.

I hadn't wanted to put a picture of my father on the boat. The thought of seeing his face fade in the sun as we rowed across the sea seemed too close a metaphoric parallel to the many years since his death. Brad was in charge of the decals, and I had not asked him to make one of my father. When I saw the photo my mother suggested, however, I changed my mind. In this photo my dad was the image of dapperness, drinking a pint and wearing a six-panel cap that had probably never gone out of style in rural England. He had brown hair, shaggy by the standards of the scale manufacturing industry, perhaps. His eyes were big and brown behind large horn-rims. They had always reminded my mom of soft, kind cow eyes. They were most unlike the blue eyes that she and I share. His facial features were mine. According to his old friends in Ireland, I had grown into "the bloody spit"—same nose, mouth, and jaw, only mine was covered by a reddish-blond beard instead of his lighter brown.

We posted him on the aft port bulkhead, outside of the cabin, visible to both the stern and bow rowers. He smiled in perpetuity, always on watch, his large beer never spilling no matter how the boat rocked. An Irish prayer, chosen by my mother, was affixed below the photo: "May the Lord keep you in his hands and never close his fist too tight."

My father was not the only ancestral icon on our boat. Greg's parents had brought an image of Greg's Italian grandfather and still-living grandmother that now graced the starboard, or opposing, side of the aft bulkhead, over the words "Andatevi, ragazzi! Buon tempo si spera!" Idiomatically this translates to "Go quickly, boys! Red sky at night, sailors' delight." The literal translation—"Go quickly, boys! One hopes for good weather"—conveys a more pragmatic tone. Greg's parents, Dave and Marie Spooner, had become the team parents, supportive to a fault with time and finances. There was hardly an official OAR Northwest event without them. Marie was quick with affection and encouragement, and she'd provided a steady supply of good Italian food at HQ—a welcome change from the oatmeal, tuna, egg and cheese sandwiches, and beer that had become our staple diet. Dave is a dentist and an ex-Navy man. Initial skepticism about the endeavor had grown into a quiet pride for his son. He possessed a wealth of advice, contacts, and connections, although all of this came with strong opinions.

Brad also had strong opinions, and he and Dave had become an unholy pair, working together furiously to get the sponsor decals on the boat three days before the race. The decals proved to be a much bigger job than anticipated—one made more difficult in these final hours by the tension that ran high between Brad and Dave. One perceived interference and the other incompetence. It had become a toxic work environment that Dylan, Greg, and I—preoccupied with our own "most important tasks"—were unavailable and unwilling to effectively mediate.

Brad's parents, down in California, had also donated a generous amount to the project. Quiet and understated, they had not wanted much—just a small sticker in remembrance of Brad's Aunt Penny and his grandmother, Mum—both of whom had died from lung cancer. Brad had mentioned this to me weeks before with little elaboration and a nostalgia that was uncommon in our interactions. Of the dozens of sponsor decals, and hundreds of names of supporters on the inside of boat, I noted that Penny and Mum had not made it on board.

———

We would be pushing off in forty-eight hours, and chaos reigned on our section of the dock as we struggled to pack the boat. Last minute adjustments and equipment purchases had pushed back our loading time. If we were not done by 3:00 PM, Woodvale would start penalizing us time.

The other crews had been packed since yesterday and appeared relaxed as they displayed their race-ready boats to family and friends. The *Commando Joe* crew was made up of current and former members of the British Army. One member, Pete Rowlings, had lost a son at sixteen from meningitis. The boat carried his image—a handsome young boy with a black ball cap—and their charity was the Meningitis Trust. The *Seven Oaks* team, four English police officers from a town and rugby team of the same name, represented many charities they had supported over the years. The *Yorkshire Warrior*, also a team of soldiers, had raised money for the British Army Benevolent Fund. Their captain, Paul Tetlow, led the crew from the Duke of Wellington's own Third Battalion the Yorkshire Regiment.

Somewhere between the side of the boat and the dock, Douglas, my younger brother, tripped. A plastic bag flew into the water and he followed it into the Hudson River. It was a wonder no one else had fallen in. Months' worth of food and hundreds of pounds of gear were being placed into the boat in some alleged order; dozens of family members, friends, and members of the Liberty Yacht Club crowded around us throughout the day. Tension and focus turned the crew into irritable creatures, incapable of managing our parents' willing hands into an effective workforce. Douglas had overheard a comment about "too many cooks in the kitchen." Still wanting to help, he had asked for an order and complied with silent industry. Dylan and I hauled him quickly from the questionable water.

"Something went in, Jordan," he said, with anger at himself. "I don't know what it was."

"Don't worry about it," I said. "Go take a shower; change your clothes." I turned to Dylan as Douglas walked up the gangplank toward the showers. "I have no idea what it could be."

Dylan surveyed the hundreds of pounds of food and other transoceanic equipment. Brad was putting the final sponsorship decals on the boat, oblivious to all but that single mission. In the frenzy of these final days, he had become, even to the three of us, impossible to talk to. He had two jobs: buying and organizing the food and affixing the sponsor decals—both of which had characteristically been left until the last minute. As usual, we were annoyed but not worried. In less than forty-eight hours we would be on the ocean. There was no time to reinventory everything to figure out what had been deep-sixed.

Dylan shrugged, clapping his hand on my shoulder. "If it's not on the boat, we don't need it, right?"

PART TWO

Greg stores desalinated water as Tropical Storm Alberto approaches.

—⌇—

Chapter 6

Exposing Ourselves
to the Sea

Day 1

The towers of the Verrazano-Narrows Bridge were visible till dusk.
Black waves topped in whitecaps grew under a bright waxing moon.
As night fell, Neil Diamond sang "America" on our boat speakers and
red-and-white fireworks exploded silently in the distance. Next to the
marina, Liberty State Park was celebrating its thirtieth anniversary.
These celebratory blasts were our last visible link to home.

My stomach twisted in nauseous discomfort after my second
shift, and I collapsed into the cabin. We'd been rowing twelve hours.
Our plan was to shift rowers every hour for the first twenty-four
before slowly extending it to two- and then three-hour shifts, rowing
day and night. We had agreed that this rotation would sustain
us across the ocean. Sacks of food and dry bags were scattered
everywhere, making the tiny cabin appear smaller and disorienting
me. The shock of the task ahead of us and the seasickness were
making everything difficult. On deck, Brad and I had rowed in the
whipping west wind, pausing to hurl ourselves to the gunwale and
vomit. Inside the cabin, and blessed with sturdy inner ears, Dylan
and Greg exchanged thankful looks, glad that the "puke pals," as
Brad dubbed us, tackled seasickness together.

—⌇—

Minutes past midnight Dylan and Greg spied a large windblown
wave growing powerfully off the stern. Empty, the boat's gunwales

sat about eight inches off the deck and about eighteen inches above the water. Hundreds of pounds of food packed tightly into our hatches for the voyage lowered our freeboard several inches. The wave gripped the hull of the boat, and the contrary North Atlantic spilled over the gunwale onto the deck.

Several miles to the northwest of our position, the same thing was happening to the smartly painted blue-and-yellow *Seven Oaks*. We had seen waves like this on the treacherous Strait of Juan de Fuca north of Washington on a training row, but this was their first time in a blow of this kind. Wave after wave surged over the side of the boat and ran through the scuppers (holes cut into the gunwale's wall where it meets the deck). It was becoming consistently harder to get the oars to clear the port side. Their hatch seals were failing.

The ocean temporarily overwhelmed our twelve scuppers as well, filling the deck like a bathtub. It took several long seconds for them to drain. The seals on our watertight hatches held, and rowers Dylan and Greg perceived no change in performance. For the first time in eighteen months since agreeing to do this crazy thing, Greg was scared. We were actually going through with it! This was not a few days in the challenging tidal waters of the Puget Sound, nor the Pacific Coast—our training cruise from Neah Bay to Grays Harbor had been dangerous, but only a few miles from land. This was open ocean, and soon we would be more than a thousand miles from land in every direction.

Somewhere closer, but just as invisible from our position, the *Yorkshire Warrior*—with the younger of the two teams of English soldiers—struggled with the same problem. They had had the shortest preparation timeline of all the teams—a little over a year compared with three years for the *Seven Oaks*, two years for the *Commando Joe*, and eighteen months for us. Combined with the challenge of having to learn to row, their arrival at the start line was extraordinary. It came with a price—a few days earlier, in the Liberty Landing boatyard, Captain Tetlow had noticed water inside the deck hatches after a torrential spring thunderstorm. They did not have time to change them. Like those of the *Seven Oaks*, the *Yorkshire Warrior's* hatches were failing.

It had taken a rainy day in Seattle six months earlier for us to figure out that the same type of hatches was no good. We had replaced them with sturdier, higher-quality ones that were four times as expensive but did not leak.

—∿∿—

By dusk of the first full day, the steady blow out of New York subsided to a gentle breeze on a docile sea. Brad and I were on deck. Our respective constitutions had improved considerably. Sunsets on the ocean seemed to be the cosmic intersection of art and nature, and the lingering haze of seasickness was not so strong that it hindered appreciation.

"I've only ever seen this in the movies," I mused. The sky stretched into blue infinity unchallenged by mountains or skyscrapers. The sun's only gown was pink and purple clouds as she began her slow descent into the sea.

"I've only ever seen the ocean in planes, flying above it," said Brad. In a plane, cruising at thirty-two thousand feet with clear skies, New York would still be visible just under two hundred miles west. From the boat all we could see was one to three miles surrounding us, depending on the sea state.

"Water, water everywhere. Not a drop to drink," I paraphrased Coleridge.

Day 3

Greg and I baked in our long-sleeved sun clothing. The water looked like a blue plain, flatter than a millpond. Only our strokes disturbed the reflection of the oar in the water.

Tropical Storm Alberto was scheduled to hit us in twenty-four hours. Both Woodvale and David Burch, our teacher turned navigator, had been following various weather forecasts. Woodvale sent storm updates via text message we received by satellite phone. David gave us a play-by-play of the storm via emails downloaded to our computer. Born in the Caribbean between the Yucatan Peninsula and Cuba, the storm made landfall on Adams Beach, Florida. It flooded areas of several southeastern states and caused the mandatory evacuation of twenty-one thousand Floridians. In North Carolina it drowned an eight-year-old boy.

After reaching near hurricane strength, Alberto had weakened considerably in its three-day 650-mile binge across land, but it had reached the ocean again just off Virginia Beach and had resumed tropical storm status. It was headed right toward us and the warm, energy-rich waters of the Gulf Stream. There was little we could do now but row. I kept track of our course by looking at the electronic compass on the bulkhead. I turned around once every five to ten minutes to scan the horizon for ships. Occasionally we rowed through patches of floating plants we dubbed "ocean tumbleweed." It was sargassum, a pelagic (free-floating), gas-filled seaweed common in many parts of the Atlantic.

I heard it first—like a rolling boil in a large pot. I stood, turning to face east. A low wall of white water from horizon to horizon rolled toward us. "What the hell is that?" I asked Greg.

"No idea," he replied groggily.

I called into the cabin. "Hey guys, you better get the camera." It moved faster than a freighter and seemed to cover the entire sea surface. Memories of tall tales mingled with a genuine fear of the unknown as I struggled to categorize what was happening.

They approached, hundreds of them, perhaps more than a thousand. Gray and black bodies undulated an arm's length from our hull. Dolphins.

"It's like they're on stampede," said Dylan.

Greg laughed, delighted by the sight.

"You can *hear* them," I said. Beneath us, surprisingly audible above the water, were the sounds of their sonar—a massive crowd of Flippers chattering to one another in happy conversation. They were stacked on top of each other, swimming swiftly with unknown intent. Until then, I would have considered ten dolphins in one place a lot. We stared, our jaws agape, as the animals swept with surreal speed into the horizon south of us.

"People could be at sea their whole lives and maybe see this a handful of times," Greg said, shaking with excitement.

They appeared to be running from something, yet they headed toward the storm. We had seen a superpod. It's a rare phenomenon where smaller pods join up deep at sea when there is an abundance of food. They were not running—they were hunting. We maintained our course east, running *away* from the weather, with the knowledge that our craft could not escape the storm's onslaught.

The dolphin stampede spoiled us. Dozens of the happy creatures continued to appear periodically throughout the day, just not in the huge numbers to which we had suddenly grown accustomed. "Dolphins again. Only ten or fifteen." The oppressive heat made movement difficult and enthusiasm impossible. For hours on end, dead calm was broken only by the clunk of oar stroke.

—◠◠◠—

Later in the day, we received a text message that *Seven Oaks*'s daggerboard had broken. After three days on the water, the thought of tackling the remaining 3027 nautical miles with busted equipment was too much. With heavy hearts the crew decided to call Mark Terry, captain of the *Sula*, for a rescue. The *Sula* was the race organizer's fifty-five-foot sailboat, tasked with looking out for the rowers in case of an emergency. This was not the way we wanted to beat *Seven Oaks*. However, a fundamental difference separated our two teams: we implicitly trusted our sturdy craft.

Day 4

Our custom-built sliding seats were completely silent. In the hot, heavy air, the only noise was the oars, our muttered complaints about the heat, and rumination on the upcoming storm.

Night passed and so did most of the next day and the storm still had not come. Nothing seemed to change. Just a blue desert with the occasional ocean tumbleweed drifting by. Waiting was miserable, but our belief that we could rely on the weather report helped. Burch assured us that Alberto was still heading straight for us. David was scary smart—once described as a guy who could build a watch to find out the time. Dylan was convinced that at the very least he knew the people who controlled the weather and could influence them.

Throughout the afternoon an essential and obnoxious hum dominated our mostly silent world. It was the sound of desalinating salt water. The unit was kept safe beneath the deck of the cabin. With its capacity to make six gallons an hour, we ran it two hours every other day to conserve our limited solar energy. This incredible device works through a process called reverse osmosis. The filtration system works on the level of salt ions. A small sturdy pump thrusts salt water through a membrane of multilayered high-tech fabric wound around a small tube. The membrane is encased in a larger tube built to withstand the high pressure required for the process. Roughly 10 percent of the water is purified as it passes through the fabric on its way to the small central tube. The rest of the water, now saltier than before, is pumped separately back into the sea.

In the afternoon a sopping rain began to fall. We finished the water-making process by storing our twelve gallons of water in rugged nylon bags, caching them in various spots around the boat. We secured everything but the oars and continued to row east over still calm water.

An artist's rendition of the storm from a third-grade class
at West Woodland Elementary School

—◠◠—

Chapter 7

In the Hands of God

And now the Storm-blast came . . .
—Samuel Taylor Coleridge,
The Rime of the Ancient Mariner

The four of us rowed under the assumption that we did not have the strength to muscle three thousand pounds of boat faster than the other teams did. The plan was to rely on our rowing experience and superior equipment to stay behind the oars longer in weather others could not or would not row in. This motivated Greg and me to keep sculling through the clouds and rising winds that prematurely darkened the evening on Day 4. Our matching red jackets turned crimson as fat raindrops and spray from waves—ten feet high and building—saturated the water-repellent fabric. The oars swung violently up and down as we struggled to keep the blades connected to the water. The unpredictable movement slammed the hardwood handles against our shins. Bursts of profanity punctuated the atmosphere. Alberto had arrived.

Brad and Dylan opened the cabin door and secured their twelve-foot lifelines before stepping out on deck and into the elements. If one of us fell out of this boat without a lifeline in the darkness and in these conditions, death would come quickly. Exposure, hypothermia, or drowning would be the end. Our vessel was simply too underpowered to maneuver quickly enough to guarantee rescue.

Greg steered the bow away from the oncoming waves. I gave the first of the three calls at the ten-, five-, and two-minute marks that signaled the shift change. Riding with the swells kept the deck as level as possible as we prepared for the switch. Dylan and I gripped each other's left forearm, which helped me out of the stern seat and him into it in a counterclockwise maneuver—a hand for the boat and a hand for each other. Once seated, Dylan leaned back and held the lines of the foot steering system in position, allowing Greg and Brad to begin a hunched catwalk on opposite sides of the deck, hands clutching the half-inch gray polymer rope that was allegedly as strong as stainless steel cable. Greg and I hastily relayed what pertinent information we had gleaned during our two hours on the oars. We sped through the usual postshift routine of stretching, peeing, and casual socializing to get under the cover of the cabin ASAP.

Greg dropped his rain pants, tore off his jacket, and dove through the hatch. I waited on deck, listening for the knuckle-on-Lexan go-ahead signal before I stripped and swung in. Lexan is one of the many supermaterials created in the 1950s. Tough, heat resistant, ultraviolet resistant, and with excellent optical qualities, it has been in everything from astronaut helmets and bullet-proof glass to high-performance yo-yos, and in this application—our boat hatches.

Thirty minutes later, the hatch opened a crack. "Too rough to row," yelled Brad. "We're deploying the sea anchor." I sighed, letting go of hopes that I would enjoy two uninterrupted hours inside an almost dry cabin. It appeared bigger than it had when we left New York, but we still needed to cram 850 pounds of crew in about thirty square feet of space.

Brad opened the door to the front cabin, and Dylan pulled out the large turquoise bag containing the sea anchor. The meager illumination from the tiny LED (light-emitting diode) deck light forced them to rely on touch to unpack the simple contraption from its bag. "Sea anchor" is a misnomer. The anchor is literally a parachute that sits under the surface of the water, creating massive drag to arrest the boat's movement. Crouched low behind the bow cabin, Dylan and Brad linked the anchor's stainless steel shackle to the rope bridle on the bow. Fighting to keep his balance on the lurching deck, Brad fed the chute into the black water, making sure the nine feet of nylon fabric and its web of lines would open properly. As the chute blossomed, he let the two hundred feet of yellow rope run loosely through his hands to prevent the coils from snagging. Simultaneously Dylan fed out the longer trip line that would collapse the chute for easy retrieval once it was calm enough to row again.

As the chute's rope went taut, the wind and waves brought the full force of the tropical storm to bear and swung the bow hard into the waves. After the tense spin and jerk, our ride smoothed immediately as the narrow bow sliced the waves instead of taking them on the full twenty-nine feet of our broadside. Brad and Dylan crawled back to the rear of the boat and collected the rest of the equipment and food we would need to make it through the storm.

Cracking the cabin's door, Brad used his body to block the waves and shoved in the last bits of safety equipment and rations. The hatch shut and we heard a disembodied debate over shedding their soaked clothing out on deck or inside the cabin.

Greg spoke. "First time I imagined this happening, I thought I would be a bit more scared, but I'm actually quite calm right now." He looked around the cabin. "The only thing I'm not looking forward to is a bunch of wet bodies getting—"

"I'm coming in!" yelled Brad, diving into the middle of the cabin, head to toe with Greg and me. As if on queue, we began whipping a naked Brad with our absorbent camp towels.

"Dry him down! Delouse him!" I yelled. Not even a tropical storm could tamp down our usual locker-room jest.

"Oh God, if that's the treatment I'm getting, I'm staying out here," called Dylan from above.

In ten minutes the waves had grown to nearly fifteen feet and higher. The cabin was already full of naked or scantily clad men. A wave crashed outside, soaking Dylan. He waited until the set passed and jumped in. "It sucks out there!"

Ribaldry filled the air. "This is a sausage fest like I've never seen," complained Greg.

A loud thump hit the cabin and the bawdy exchange ceased. Water sloshed next to the hull and the white noise of the rain intensified as we listened for a corresponding sound that signaled breakage.

"Is that an inside sound or an outside sound?" asked Greg cautiously. Tonight could turn into one of our worst-case scenarios.

—⁓—

After traveling over water for a day and a half since almost dying on land, the storm had regained more than its original strength. It approached us at just under hurricane strength. The boat, locked down in the waves with the sea anchor, was invisible in the dark. Even if we had enough power for radar, using it to detect any oncoming ships was not a viable option. Our boat was so low to the water that each radio signal, especially in a storm like this, would reflect off the nearest waves and return a useless signal. We did have an active radar responder. When it got pinged by an oncoming ship, the device would signal back, but this too was hindered by wave height and the earth's curvature.

In lieu of radar, safety required two men on deck constantly scanning the horizon. Ships were identified visually, contacted on the VHF radio, and notified of our position and vector. In the dark, in a storm, and on sea anchor, no one was on deck. Traveling through one of the busiest shipping lanes in the world, we faced a real possibility of collisions. Being mowed down by a larger vessel was the worst of our worst-case scenarios. If we were hit during the storm, it would be sudden and completely unexpected. We would have no time to prepare. Holed up in the unbearably clammy hot box of a cabin, sweating profusely, we chose the calculated risk of keeping our survival gear close, but not actually putting it on, to try and rest. If we were hit—and in the unlikely event we survived—we would be completely exposed to the elements.

The second worst of our worst-case scenarios was flipping in immense storm waves. Eight of the nine rowboats that had previously attempted to cross the North Atlantic from the United States had capsized at some time during their journey. The only boat that did not was a Dutch crew rowing a boat similar to ours the summer before. If our mistakes were limited, the hull would roll upright no worse for wear. We could be thrown and cartwheeled, but unless we hit something harder than us, we would float like a cork. Still a frightening prospect, it was less deadly than a collision.

Nervous breathing staled the air. I looked at the open vent above my head and at the one above Brad. Airflow was a necessity, but opening the vents compromised the cabin's airtight chamber and the boat's ability to self-right. A rope was attached to the vent and could be pulled at a moment's notice. If the vents were kept closed, we would eventually pass out. We left them open, assuming that if we flipped, we would have the presence of mind to pull them shut.

The craft was equipped with a four-man rubber life raft lashed to the deck. If we overturned and the boat did not right itself, our best course of action would be to deploy the raft and lash it to our boat. The unofficial rule of thumb is that a crew steps into a life raft only when the deck of their vessel is below the surface. Either we would wait out the storm and try to salvage our boat in calmer water, or activate our EPIRB (emergency position-indicating radio beacon). The beacon would send a distress signal to a satellite and then to all boats in the area, the closest of which we hoped would respond. It could be hours or days.

———

Back in our buffeted, claustrophobic cabin, the memory of our open-ocean emergency drill with the Seattle Maritime Academy obsessed me. I waited for a lull in the conversation and then said, "Just so we do have a plan... you know... worst-case-scenario type thing. Um... " I paused, pairing my concern with a casual tone. "Say we have to abandon. We'll start with alphabetical order. I guess we would be starting with Brad. Get him into his clothes and into his dry suit first. Then work through Dylan, Greg, and then me."

"Okay," Dylan acknowledged. The others nodded.

"Get each person completely outfitted, and if it's practical to get 'em out of the cabin, great; if not, then whatever. We have that set order to go by. Everybody helps everybody get ready as fast as they can." I had no plan beyond this. How could we repeat what we had done at the SMA here in the dark, amid twenty-five-foot waves? Wind howled throughout the evening, with sustained winds of sixty miles per hour and gusts up to eighty. A half inch of fiberglass separated us from unadulterated wild. I wondered how far the flat white light of our cabin's LED could be seen in the ebony void beyond. We listened to the metronome-like static feedback of the VHF radio. What else might be close by?

I lay facing the bulkhead, the unseen tempest raging an inch from my face. Fat tropical raindrops bombarded the hull like tiny kamikaze planes. Their strikes on the composite surface sounded like a plastic grocery bag crumpled close to my ear.

Roaring swells tore past us, pulling the boat downwind, the hull moving as if on the end of a whip. It seemed that every fifteen minutes a wave bigger than all previous swells rocked the boat. Each hit provoked fear and wonder. As long as they came at the bow, the large swells rolled under us. Coming from the beam, they knocked the broadside of the boat like a titanic prizefighter slamming the hull more than seventy degrees. Only the boat's cylindrical shape and heavy ballast of food, equipment, and emergency water kept the hull from completing its roll.

Each of us had found spots in the cabin to brace ourselves. Without opening our eyes, our arms shot out to the nearest bulkhead. The rapid pendulum motion of the huge waves threatened to turn the cabin into a front-loading washing machine. After five days of ten- to ninety-minute naps in two-hour shifts, we were exhausted. Still, no one could find rest as the hours drifted by.

I was homesick for each speck of dirt, every restaurant in Seattle, and crisp, clean cotton sheets. However, even in this sticky, sweaty, terrifying moment, the fact remained that I was living the dream. Miserable as this was, we had fought tooth and nail for this privilege. It tempered my fear and any urge to feel sorry for myself.

I was surprised to find out later that Dylan had been silently reciting the Serenity Prayer throughout the ordeal. God, despite the lack of a formal invitation, had become quite present. Regardless of our levels of faith and skepticism, we all welcomed and were moved mightily by the daily prayers that arrived via text message. My personal favorite, from my Grandma Evie and delivered through my Aunt Lola, was that she was "storming heaven" for our safe passage. It had felt right to have a priest bless our boat back on the dock in Liberty Landing Marina, and the Irish prayer my mother had penned below the picture of my dad was made for a storm at sea.

—◊◊◊—

A waxy sheen of respiration and condensed sweat covered everything in the cabin. In the early hours of morning but well before dawn, a sound like a freight train rocking precariously off its tracks thundered off port side. Like a giant, it seized our boat in massive hands, lifting us only to drop us back to the sea. My hand went to close the tiny vent as water forced its way into the cabin. Cold ocean mingled with the sweat on my face.

Dawn revealed gray water and white skies as we began peeking tentatively out of the cabin. The worst of the wind had abated, but the waves still looked like hills the size of two-story houses rolling under and past us. Compelled to document what was going on, I pulled out the video camera. "Everybody's in pretty good spirits," I reported. "But both the rudder cables snapped, and right now we hear a very unpleasant thump-thump of the rudder hitting the stoppers in the stern." "Unpleasant" was an understatement. Each thump sounded like a Hell's Angel taking a two-by-four to the hull.

The stoppers were fabricated plastic blocks that kept the carbon-fiber rudder from whipping the transom of the boat apart. Dylan had built them on a suggestion from Dan Heyl at Emerald Harbor Marine. Dan was our electric systems guru; without him, the boat could do little more than float. We observed any of his "suggestions" as orders. As we lay in the stern of the boat, the slam of the rudder on the resilient plastic stoppers instead of our hull confirmed that our trust in Larry and Dan had been well founded.

—⁓—

Hours later, it still raged too hard to row. After hundreds of waves, we could anticipate the bubbly swirl of a wave that would roll under the hull from the crashing sound that preceded it. After one of these waves hit, there would be a brief pause as the entire cockpit was submerged below churning water before the scuppers drained it off. I opened the hatch between a set of waves. After eight hours in the cabin, the fresh air felt like stepping into a cold shower on a muggy summer day.

"Cross breeze," said Greg, sighing after each deep breath.

"Oh wow, that's what we needed," said Dylan.

For a few brief seconds, we enjoyed a temperature approaching normal. Then I heard the crash of a wave and quickly shut the hatch. Water deflected off the Lexan. The cabin temperature rose again, and I listened for the next set of clean waves that would allow us the luxury of airflow.

"It's like I paid someone forty thousand dollars to take me to a sauna," said Greg. "A shitty, cramped sauna."

"With nothing but a rowing machine and a whip," I added.

—⁓—

The storm finally abated enough that Brad was willing to try his luck relieving himself beyond our one-liter pee bottle. This was one carefully marked item. The discomfort of this task in the cabin had kept us from drinking water as liberally as we should have, and we were all dehydrated. Brad's eagerness to get on deck was a chance to get a real assessment of the storm. It also gave us the opportunity to have one fewer body in the cabin, if only for a bit.

Brad had always functioned on his own schedule—we dubbed it "Brad time." At various periods during the eighteen months of preparation, our feelings on "Brad time" ranged from slight irritation (at his shaving ten minutes before a downtown sponsorship meeting) to total amazement (at his infuriating habit of accomplishing a week's work in an all-nighter). Tropical storm be damned, Brad was on his own schedule. He whooped in defiance at the abating storm. The wind whipped at his rain-slicked hair and knocked frothy white foam off the tops of the twenty-foot waves. Brad locked the video camera down in its mount to film the next few dramatic moments.

He called into the cabin amid the salt spray. "I'm going to take a dump—are there any wet wipes?" The head was a white five-gallon bucket with no seat. It was attached to the boat with a string and a carabiner. Next to it was a toilet brush, also attached with another string and carabiner. We had a hatch full of wet wipes, and the contents of the bucket were washed into the sea. It was that simple.

For twelve long minutes Brad tried to relax, hoping a wave would not knock him off the bucket. High winds had cleared the sky of clouds, and the waves turned electric blue in the sun. It was a disconcerting but beautiful day. Brad succeeded in his task and returned to the cabin, noting that the sliding seat on our boat had nearly destroyed our bucket. Luckily, we had brought a spare.

—⁓—

An hour later the wind died down to a brisk twenty-five knots. David would later confirm using satellite images that the actual wind speed in our location had exceeded seventy-five knots, well into hurricane strength. The waves lost their driving power, sloshing erratically like water in a bathtub full of toddlers. After being cooped up with three large, sweaty men for the better part of twenty-four hours, I anticipated rowing as I would a vacation. Every bit of equipment, including ourselves, had performed as expected. Even the rudder stoppers—the source of those disturbing bumps in the night— showed almost no wear.

More clouds had blown our direction and the water changed its color to a gray-blue. Greg and I took the first turn back on the oars, happy to give Brad and Dylan a few hours of real rest. The surprisingly stable boat crested the tops of the waves, allowing us to see for miles before we slid into the troughs, where walls of water created a temporary world no wider than a hundred yards. This was the ocean I had imagined.

It was important to us to document what we were doing; not a day went by that we did not shoot at least an hour of HD film.

—∿∿—

Chapter 8

Leaving Ithaca

Day 9

Four days had passed since Alberto, and each night our oars glowed green with eerie beauty. Every splash lit up the hull with a V of light, and unknown sea beasts darted in spectral luminosity. The energy of each disturbance causes chemicals in the plankton (several hundred per liter) to light up in one of nature's most delightful expressions. This was bioluminescence, and the reality surpassed what I had imagined.

Now lightning fractured the dark purple sky while waves and wind, subdued compared to the violent heavens, urged us gently to England. The light show had traveled to the sky. Greg and Brad, in matching black long underwear, braced themselves against the cabin bulkhead on the aft deck and brooded over the spectacular lightning. I observed from my perch out the stern hatch. Brad asked how I was feeling. I paused before croaking an answer. "I'm sweaty, I'm covered in salt, and the only time that's good for me is when I'm rowing."

Six hours earlier, the decision to stop had seemed prudent as inky night threatened to crack apart on top of us. Predawn's glow enabled us to better gauge the distance of the danger, making the night's resolution to stop seem indulgent as we calculated the miles lost.

Lightning was an indication that we were on course for the Gulf Stream. Our central navigational strategy was to follow it. Lightning on the ocean is infrequent when compared to occurrences on land, but the weather crossing the Gulf Stream results in as many strikes per square mile as the thunderstorm-prone plains of the midwestern United States.

Getting the rowers off the deck and into the cabin seemed sensible, but the effect was more of a mental salve than a practical solution. Dan Heyl, our electrician, had chosen not to ground the vessel. If we were unlucky enough to get hit, he had told us bluntly, grounding would not make a damn bit of difference. If hit, we would experience an electrical shock, followed by a hole burned into some part of the boat as lightning coursed through the hull. If we did not die, every system would likely be fried. We turned off our electronics, which wouldn't do much, but the gesture made us feel safer. On the chance that we would survive this theoretical calamity, it was doubtful we could finish the race with only our backup hand-powered water maker (same concept as the electric, just smaller and hand-powered) and novice skill with the sextant.

Made mostly from wood, our oars—custom built for greater efficiency and durability—were wrapped in a highly conductive sleeve of carbon-fiber fabric. It seemed prudent to take these lightning rods out of our hands, although this precaution was yet another illusion of safety. The other teams' oars were made entirely of carbon, and we assumed they shared our sense of self-preservation and suffered similarly, waiting out the lightning storm.

—∿∿—

A day before the lightning storm appeared, my girlfriend, Rebecca, had sent me an email. There was a paradox in receiving and answering emails beamed from a satellite as we rowed a boat across the ocean. Although most of the time the messages from moms, dads, and girlfriends proved a comfort, the privilege of easy communication was a double-edged sword. For example Nick Edwards, who was looking after my house (aka OAR Northwest HQ) and keeping it rented, wrote me for advice on what model replacement dryer to buy. I'm not sure what that says about the state of high adventure in the twenty-first century.

Rebecca had quoted Homer's *Odyssey* in her email: "Fit out a ship with twenty oars, the best in sight, and sail in quest of news of your long-lost father." This was advice from the Greek goddess Athena to Odysseus's son, Telemachus. Rebecca had a knack for sending quotations, and this one touched me most. I felt a kinship with the young Greek hero. His father, like mine, had been gone for twenty years. Both Odysseus and Jim Hanssen had a love of travel, but Telemachus would eventually find news that his father was alive. I suspect the *Odyssey* would have been very different with a satellite phone.

The incoming text messages—the only electronic convenience we allowed ourselves in the storm—reminded us that it was Father's Day. Messages kept coming in saying, "James Robert Hanssen must be very proud." It felt good to hear it but not wholly right. After my father's death, my mom and I kept living. She eventually met another man—Jim Wood—and he became my father too. I wrote a response on weatherproof notebook paper and after the lightning passed, I posted the blog. "I know he is proud," I wrote, "because my father now is proud. His name is James Roy Wood and when he married my mom, I became his 'instant five-year-old.' I could have a dad and a stepdad, but that never felt right to me. Nature or nurture, I would not be who I am without both of them, and I am so proud to be their son."

My mother responded quickly to this. "You made Dad cry today," she wrote. "He could hardly speak. That's now the second time I've seen Dad cry. The first was the day you left. You made him feel like the most important man in the world."

In the eighteen years Jim Wood had been in my life, he had built a loving marriage with my mother. This relationship sometimes included holding her when a relic from the past cut open old grief. He never showed any sign of ego or insecurity at the mention of Jim Hanssen's name. The impact that Jim Wood's introduction into my life had on me now makes Athena's advice to Telemachus seem less relevant. Athena told him to go to sea in search of news of his father, knowing that Odysseus would already be back in Ithaca before Telemachus returned. Athena had to get Telemachus off the island, or suitors who pursued his mother Penelope would kill him. Luckily my family did not suffer that kind of drama. Telemachus and I had both gone to sea in search of information, only to realize that what we had perceived lost was at home.

During hours on the oars, staring in near delirium at the picture of Jim Hanssen on the rear cabin bulkhead, I realized this Father's Day was the beginning of my enlightenment. Alone with my thoughts and surrounded by the best oarsmen in sight.

—⁓—

Later that morning the lightning strikes seemed far enough away for us to pull out the computer, and Dylan read a race report from our navigator David Burch. "We're one hundred miles ahead of the *Yorkshire Warrior* and eighty miles ahead of the *Commando Joe.*"

"By drifting and no work we've enlarged our lead?" asked Greg.

Dylan shook his head. "They're going to be in this soon. We're going to be in cold water, and they're going to catch up to us. All the advantage we're getting right now from this drifting is going to be theirs soon." As the Gulf Stream meanders in a general northeastward direction across the North Atlantic, it is surrounded by cold water, which we would soon be in as the other teams entered the warm water and faster current.

Dylan and I set out to row while the wind was still at our backs. Nearly six hundred miles from land, the ocean and clouds seemed to imitate hills and mountains. Rain burst forth. It tasted sweet and washed away the sweat from the night in the cabin. On my starboard, the morning light radiated through the rain shower as it hit the ocean, creating golden filigree over the waves—a brilliant background to the rainbow reaching off our boat and into the sky.

Day 10

"After a hard two hours behind the oars," I said, "there's nothing quite like taking your pants off." Dylan and I lay in the cabin going out of our minds. Par for the course as, subjected to at least two shifts a day, our bodies declared mutiny. Eventually a cease-fire would be reached between the body and the mind, and the punch-drunk fever would fade to a dull ache. The weather cleared to blue sky just in time for Greg and Brad to row. Dylan and I had spent most of our shift in a windy, rainy squall, the only evidence of which was our waterlogged bodies.

"I'm not wearing a single piece of clothing," piped Dylan. It was true. He was buck-naked.

"It's just, you've got to dry off," I said to Dylan, exasperated. "You're constantly damp. Today opened up and everything's wet. In here, we're still damp. Our fingers are pruning. There's nothing you can do. You don't want your junk to stay wet for days 'cause funky shit happens."

Lewis and Clark had observed a similar phenomenon two hundred years earlier with the Clatsop tribe at the mouth of the Columbia River. After thousands of years living on the water in the damp Pacific Northwest, these Native Americans had discovered that no pants is really the best way to go if you are in a state of constant dampness.

It was no joke. The necessity of taking our pants off every time we finished rowing was losing hilarity. Routine had set in and as the novelty faded, the gauche realities of boat life were grim. Damp spandex under rain pants exacerbated a variety of "downstairs" disorders. Going pantless was not foolproof, however. Dylan, despite strict adherence to the no-pants rule, would succumb to one of these ailments, igniting fear that a virulent undercarriage contagion might exist on the cabin's blue foam floor.

For now, this was not an issue, and Dylan eagerly discussed his excitement at reaching the two-digit mark. Ten days at sea. "A week's a big deal. But ten days? It's like we could be a sixth of the way done with this whole thing." We had traveled over 611 miles since leaving New York, and spent more than twenty-four hours in foul weather that had forced us to sit it out on sea anchor. Even with Burch's intelligence, we had grossly underestimated the size and complexity of the Gulf Stream. Our lack of oceanic experience and profusion of optimism had inspired a week's worth of false positives. Although greatly sobered to the difficulty of catching the Gulf Stream in a rowboat, we still expected it any day now.

The Gulf Stream's warm, meandering course throws off huge eddies that become independent patches of current unattached from the main stream. Navigating depended on figuring out the location and direction of the eddies and our position within them. Then we could decide how long it would be productive to ride the current. David instructed us to stop every two hours and do a drift test to augment the weather charts. Lightning-fast speed for us was five knots, so one-half- to three-knot currents could be decisive. Over the next day or so, we expected the *Yorkshire Warrior* to gain on us. We delved ahead into slow, cold water, continuing the search for the Gulf Stream while the competition would row into the favorable eddy that we had experienced the day before.

"Who cares *how* we're in the lead," Dylan said. "It's *that* we're in the lead that counts." His fanaticism with winning was a new development. Most of the time he was putting things into perspective for the rest of us. "If we're losing, it's not just the race that we're losing. It's us somehow invalidating everything we've done over the last year and a half."

It was not a healthy attitude, but it was irresistible. We measured our self-worth by how much we could sacrifice to this venture. The project was our siren. During moments of clarity we dreamed of a future without obsession. There was no compensation for working this hard, no prize money. Just pure, unsustainable mania to see it to the end, knowing that however this adventure turned out, it would be the hardest thing we had ever done. The row had opened up a reservoir of power that none of us had previously tapped. Zealots that we were, bold enough to believe in ourselves, we still measured ourselves against others to validate these sacrifices. To not see results of our labors translated to a win would crush us. A prophecy unfulfilled.

Day 12

Twelve days out of New York, *Sula*'s sail appeared on the horizon. As it approached, skipper Mark Terry and his crew furled sails to slow their speed. They cruised up and down the crests and troughs of the white-capping eight-foot waves and—quite literally—made circles around us as we exchanged news and enjoyed the civilized pleasantries of company on a lonely sea.

Greg maneuvered the boat for a specific camera shot that had proven elusive thus far. "Jesus Christ," I said, "are we going to try mooning again?"

All serendipity had gone. A third and, I hoped, final attempt would be made to catch the "full broad side" of Dylan's and my rump. The first two passes had failed to get captured on film. All seven souls occupying this lonely patch of the North Atlantic had become oddly and enthusiastically invested in getting perfect footage of a "mooning on the high seas." On Greg's mark, Dylan and I in unison shipped our oars across the gunwales, dropped trou, and brought to bare the maximum gluteal barrage. Cheers erupted. Mission accomplished.

A dashing if slightly gangly figure in the cockpit of the *Sula*, Mark had news to share: a week earlier, the *Yorkshire Warrior* had lost its daggerboard. His chipper English accent described what must have been a horrifying situation. "On the night of the gale they picked up a fishing line or long line or some net." The VHF radio squelched and screeched over his voice. "Got hooked around it and they got wrapped round and round . . . it pulled the daggerboard right out of the boat."

During Tropical Storm Alberto, the *Sula* had positioned itself equidistant between the three crews in anticipation of a distress signal. The *Yorkshire Warrior*, after the crew deployed their sea anchor, got its daggerboard entangled with some type of metal fishing buoy, damaging a spare oar and some of the deck. To untangle it, one of the crew dove into the water to cut away the loose rope with a knife. Their one and only daggerboard had been destroyed. The fact that this did not also damage the hull irreparably seemed a miracle.

Terror plagued the *Yorkshire Warrior* as the crew realized that their unreliable deck hatches were taking on too much water. It became necessary to have shifts of one man sitting outside throughout the storm pumping like mad. The *Sula* made its way to them, circling to see if they would need assistance, though it would come with disqualification. Then the *Sula* itself became endangered, and Mark began to wonder if it was his boat that would need rescuing. "Our wind[-powered] generator was blown from the back of the boat." He went on to list the catastrophes that inundated them. "Our guard wires had broken . . . lost a lot of gas . . . developed a leak . . . . " He concluded that they endured "a lot of epics that night." After a pause, he politely asked, "I'm sure you guys had a bit of a struggle too, eh? Did you have a good night's sleep?"

Steering the boat with one hand and speaking into the VHF with the other, Mark continued. "I bet it was cozy. But you did well. Better than the rest of the boats, in fact. Obviously what you did in your preparations was good. It's a credit to you, really, and now it's all paying off nicely."

It was a big compliment coming from Mark, a man who had crossed the Atlantic in a sailboat thirteen times. Our mutual respect had grown in leaps and bounds since the race had begun. In addition to being the race boat skipper, Mark and the other Woodvale crew members were responsible for making sure the boats met race regulations. *Sula*'s crew could tell from our boat that there had been plenty of thought put into the actual rowing apparatus. On land, this was all they thought we had going for us. Our obsessive attitude had appeared as utter chaos and had given them doubts about our readiness. Mark and the crew would later admit they had placed a private bet on us—a bottle of booze—based entirely upon our equipment.

"You using your autopilot at all?" Mark asked. We had yet to use the autopilot and told him as much.

There was a moment of stunned silence on the VHF. "Yeah, okay," Mark finally said. "We thought you might be using it due to the fact you were steering in such a straight line and had such a good course. But obviously you were just rowing very, very well." Mark stuck around long enough to catch our shift change on film. Later he posted his official daily race report on Woodvale's website: "Just caught up with the OAR Northwest crew. They are in great form, stayed with them for just about one hour. You can see why they are in such a good position—the drive and enthusiasm is great. They did not stop rowing the whole time we were there."

———

Despite losing their daggerboard, the *Yorkshire Warrior* was keeping a proverbial stiff upper lip. They were making significant gains as we searched in vain for the Gulf Stream. The *Yorkshire*'s misfortune was another confirmation that we were right to make no assumptions when it came to our safety on the water. The poorly made daggerboards were one of many reasons our relationship with Woodvale had soured. The *Commando Joe* had also broken its daggerboard on a training cruise, and like us, they'd built another one. We were angry with Woodvale. To have known the daggerboards were weak well before the start of the race and not insist the other teams take a spare (or have them rebuilt) seemed irresponsible. It had been a contributing factor to the retirement of the *Seven Oaks* and now, despite some gains, the *Yorkshire Warrior* had one fewer tool with which to face the North Atlantic.

Woodvale Events (now called Atlantic Campaigns) was initially The Challenge Business when it put together the first official ocean-rowing race in 1997, founded by the celebrated British adventurer Chay Blyth. Blyth and John Ridgeway, the second team to row the North Atlantic since George Harbo and Frank Samuelsen in 1896, had made their voyage in 1966. Despite living in the atomic age, with radar reflectors, VHF radio, and search planes, Blyth and Ridgeway's feat—their ninety-two-day trip to the west coast of Ireland—was still considered impossible at the time. They were awarded the British Empire Medal for their efforts. Chay later sold the business to Simon Chalk, an ex-participant turned entrepreneur in his midtwenties. Simon created mid-Atlantic ocean rows on a biannual basis. By the time OAR Northwest began expressing interest, Simon had started to expand competitions to the North Atlantic and the Indian Ocean.

By the time of our race Simon had rowed the mid-Atlantic twice and become the first rower across the Indian Ocean. Simon had several other ocean rows planned in the future, but he was currently working on a solo trimaran "wrong-way-round" circumnavigation of the world, funded partially by a rowdy quayside late-night dance club. ("Wrong way" refers to making the trip east to west and against predominant weather patterns—a feat requiring a very tough boat.)

Needless to say, during the preceding eighteen months Simon had been a little distracted. Our direct contact with him had been limited to a half dozen emails. Being a transatlantic ticket away, our Seattle location precluded face-to-face meetings that might have mitigated some of our communication problems. Under Simon's leadership with Woodvale Events, the number of ocean rowers has increased exponentially. At the very least, I had Simon to thank for that poster sent to the Lake Washington Rowing Club halfway around the world.

Sula's good-humored visit had been a step forward in repairing the trust between Woodvale and our team. Hearing about the crews' bravery during the storm showed us that whatever faults Woodvale may have had on land, when push came to shove, Mark and his crew were in a small boat in a big ocean and would do anything to help us if we called.

—⁓—

That afternoon the boat rolled drunkenly in the seas. I felt a light jerk followed by uneasy looseness in my hand. A wave of nausea overwhelmed me as I realized what had happened. The third thole pin in fewer than three days had broken, less than a thousand miles into the trip. It was impossible to row a boat conventionally without them. If the oar was a lever, this finger-thick stainless steel pin was the fulcrum. A black oarlock fit on top of the thole pin, allowing it to swivel with each stroke. Made of resilient nylon, it had a stainless steel clasp on top that locked the oar in place. As the boat tipped to and fro, the oar would sometimes get stuck in the water. Most of the time it broke free without issue, but now the thole pins seemed to be snapping with disturbing regularity. Four new pins had been installed in New Jersey. Although I had asked the crew for input, *I* was responsible for getting the riggers made and deciding how many spares to bring. As they were heavy, I had felt two per rigger was plenty.

It took almost thirty minutes in the rocking boat to change the pin. Dylan was silent. This could jeopardize the row. To counteract the problem, someone suggested we row with the oarlock gates open, allowing the oar to tear free of the rigger instead of breaking the boat. This release of the oar happened almost every other stroke in bad waves, forcing us to stop and put the oar back in place. A feeling of despair overwhelmed me. Would the team's potential failure fall squarely on my shoulders?

Day 14

One-hour-on, one-hour-off had been our strategy for sprinting out of New York. Over the first thirty-six hours we'd extended this to an hour-and-half and then to two hours, where we'd sat for two weeks. On our Pacific training row we'd practiced three-hours-on, three-hours-off. We had not adjusted our shifts yet to gain the final hour. I knew—and I thought the crew agreed—that the minimum sleep we would need to sustain our effort was at least three hours, to reach a full cycle of rapid eye movement (REM) sleep. Achieving this state of deep sleep is critical to health. It takes ninety minutes to get to the first REM cycle, which typically lasts about five to ten minutes. This was almost impossible to do on our current schedule. I had convinced myself that if we did not add this last hour, we would eventually come up against a wall.

Although we strived to reach consensus on each issue, my role as captain was tiebreaker (I had two votes). I laid out my case, but I was outvoted. My credibility had been broken, like the snapping thole pins. My personal state was beyond tired, and if I could not convince the crew we needed a different sleep schedule, I doubted that I could lead when they might need me to. I felt alone on the tiny boat, finding solace in emails from Rebecca, my mother, and Nick. I prayed for my body to adjust.

A midday snooze in the back cabin wearing rain gear

—◦◦◦—

Chapter 9

Low on Fuel

Day 16

Brad stood naked on deck and put on his safety harness. Laundry covered the boat, drying in afternoon sun and placid seas. Dylan and Greg slept down below. With the monotone voice of resigned exhaustion, I narrated for the video camera: "Brad is going to check out the underside of the boat. Going to look for some..."

"Sharks, first," he said, making a casual reference to the eight-foot blue shark that had glided lazily past our oars the day before.

"Sharks, looking for sharks first," I echoed. There were miles of water between us and the sea floor, with untold numbers of ocean beasts wriggling in between. I wasn't happy with Brad's decision to hop in the water while we were trying to catch the Gulf Stream, but he had brought up a valid reason for a swim. Some significant growth may have appeared on the hull after sixteen days. If so, a good cleaning would decrease our drag, and pulling this boat through the ocean might become a tiny bit easier.

Brad took his time getting ready, then inspected his crotch. If he didn't find anything on the hull, "I'm going to clean off the underside of *my* boat." He laughed at his own joke. Looking at the water and then back at the camera, Brad spoke in a strange tone, "It's the most unnatural thing in the world to step off this boat." He jumped.

Day 17

The next morning Brad had become a different person. His joviality from the previous day was gone, replaced by a sullen, morose mood. Dylan and Greg were on deck. It was noon when Brad spoke up from the other side of the cabin. "I need to talk to you about the food." I'd been trying to doze; this caught my attention. Brad's concerned tone plus the subject matter plus rowing in the middle of the North Atlantic could only mean one thing: we might not have enough food.

An inappropriate, selfish sense of relief coursed through my body. I realized this would replace the breaking thole pins as the issue du jour. This feeling was followed by empathy: this was bad, and the level of badness was unknown. I should have felt angry but was not—I could not find the energy to care about anything but the solution. In measured, tired tones, I asked how this could have happened. Brad explained that it had taken him almost two weeks to recognize the problem and a couple of days to process it and acknowledge that he had to say something.

My final and strongest emotion was fear—not of starvation, but of plummeting crew morale. This could tear us apart. I was especially worried about Greg and Brad. The tension between them had seemed to mellow the first week on the water, but it had returned with a vengeance since then. In Greg's opinion, Brad was selfish and had disappointed the team on multiple occasions. "If something needs to be done for the team," Greg had said of Brad, "it's 'hold on, I gotta get my shit done first.'"

What it came down to was a lack of chemistry. Days after Brad had moved into OAR Northwest headquarters, Greg expressed to me privately the suspicion that, like a house full of women with their menstrual cycles syncing up, some kind of primal male pheromone equivalent had been unleashed. Greg confessed he felt more aggressive than he had in years, an assessment I had chalked up to a biology class Greg was taking for physical therapy school. The tension often manifested itself in cruel banter from Greg. Teasing at the house was certainly sanctioned group therapy, but I felt Greg sometimes took the mockery a bit too far. Brad resented the bullying—that was obvious. Greg was four years his senior and a role model long before being a teammate. Seeing a guy he looked up to become an ass to him gave Brad a reason to shut Greg out, which compounded their less-than-cohesive communication styles.

Well before leaving Seattle, Greg and Dylan could see that I was also having a tough time with Brad. There had been an increase in little pissing matches. I understood Greg's complaints about Brad, but I also commiserated with Brad about his frustrations with Greg. He and I had been closest the longest. I felt like the middle child, constantly trying to keep the peace and to keep their energy focused on rowing across the ocean.

Dylan, for his part, floated above the daily bickering, coming down from his Zen mountaintop every once in a while to mediate or dispense the wisdom of one who listens more than he speaks. Yet during our training cruises in Puget Sound, all differences seemed to evaporate, leading us to the optimistic if naïve conclusion that maybe Dylan was right: "Once we're rowing, it's just going to be great." The last month before the race, the final preparations had taken us to the breaking point. Brad himself admitted that the way he dealt with it had alienated a lot of people. The pressure had made him difficult to work with and unreceptive to help or criticism, leaving us to trust blindly in his abilities.

—⁓—

We had a lot to worry about without the additional burden of wondering about food stores. Our days-long search for the Gulf Stream had cost us our hard-fought hundred-mile lead. If we could find it and pick up its one- to three-knot current for nearly five hundred miles, we would be well on our way to England with perhaps more than double what we had lost.

Cabin acoustics were such that all conversations on deck could be heard in the cabin, but not the other way around. Brad and I discussed the problem freely. No easy way existed for him to break the news.

With roughly ten minutes until the end of Dylan and Greg's shift, Brad moved outside the cabin. I hunkered down on my lumpy blue dry-bag, uncomfortable but not enough to want to move, and painfully aware of my procrastination. Forcing myself to the hatch, feeling very un-captain-like, I prepared to announce that Brad had something to say. I should be there to help absorb some of the fallout. Fortunately, I could make the announcement with very little energy.

Our routine was to switch rowing partners every four days to keep the company as fresh as possible. Ninety-six hours working, sleeping, and eating with the same person tried one's patience in the best of circumstances. It was the end of my four-day shift with Brad. Just before he confessed publicly, I decided to forget about the shift change—Dylan and Greg would need a day to let their anger subside. Even given the level of frustration I felt with Brad, Dylan and Greg could be assumed to have that resource in spades. If their reactions were severe enough or the resulting anger too great, I feared the team might be destroyed.

Dylan and Greg rowed in silence as Brad told them everything. When they finally spoke, the reserved nature of their statements of shock, disappointment, and anger astounded me. Brad had thought long and hard about what he was going to say. His explanations had made an impact, his self-abasement painfully complete. I wondered how I would have acted if I had to drop a bomb like that.

Later, Brad spoke in his video diary about telling the guys: "Judgment will be based largely on the outcome, and that's going to be determined by factors I do not control. That scares me, but it's a consequence, a reality I'm willing to live with. As far as the guys are concerned, apology and explanation of how we got here— useless right now." While the rest of us were in shock, Brad was able to move right into coping—he had to. He feared the most difficult apology to make would be back home, to all of our parents for his role in jeopardizing our safety.

Greg could not even talk about it. When he did, it was privately in a video diary. He was absolutely livid. "If there's ever been a bigger screwup," he said, "this is it. It all comes down to poor planning. Poor execution. Lack of responsibility." I was impressed and somewhat worried by Greg's ability to suppress his anger. He confessed to me that he would never work with Brad again. But until we could get to shore, Greg would have to.

Dylan was furious. Brad's mistake was a personal betrayal. Dylan had gone to bat for Brad back on food-packing day. Greg's parents, Dave and Marie Spooner, had been frantic at the apparent lack of any organization and had lined up family friends to help pack the food. Yet nothing seemed to be happening. Brad had been up all night running to one twenty-four-hour grocery store after another. Observing the growing concern of the Spooners, Dylan had stepped in to assure them. "It may not look like he has a plan, or sound like he has a plan, but he's spent weeks on this. He's going to get it done, and it's going to be done great." In the end, even stoic and skeptical Dave Spooner agreed Brad pulled it off. Dylan had also stepped up to defend Brad's last-minute handling of the sponsorship decals. His anger was strong but so was his optimism and compassion. In his video diary that afternoon, Dylan asserted that he would not let this ruin our success—nor his relationship with Brad.

Satellite images indicated the Gulf Stream was just around the corner. Considering its fickle nature, we could not spare the several hours it would take to inventory the food until we had confirmation we were well within the current. Until then, nothing—not even the nagging reality of a food shortage—would keep us from rowing. Days of searching fruitlessly for the famed current, coupled with the food problem, continued to devastate morale. Bagging the Gulf Stream route and changing to the more direct Great Circle route had become a serious consideration. The day was hot, and the water was the customary deep blue from midday sun. Everyone avoided lunch. I ran scenario after worst-case scenario through my head.

Brad spent a lot of time in the cabin that afternoon, wracking his brain to figure out what had gone wrong. Yet in the middle of the ocean, the why and the how mattered little compared to managing the crisis. I spent the morning on deck, leaving him alone with his thoughts. All I needed to know to calculate our next steps was how much food we had on board.

By late afternoon I had worked myself into a quiet panic. Either we rowed in silence or I listened to Brad analyze his mistakes and make overtures to amend. It was driving me mad. We had picked up some sort of strong current but dared not call it the Gulf Stream. Above us, against a five-knot wind out of the east, appeared a beautiful white bird out of nowhere. Its feathers brilliant white with two long black tails extending out the back, the bird had a pointed ocher beak and delicate, feminine features. It hovered above us, dancing gracefully before heading directly into the wind. Perhaps it was an omen.

"It can't be bad," said Brad.

I agreed. Like the early mariners, I let faith take hold, unable to shake the power of a sign.

After our shift I checked the satellite phone for text messages. Our navigator, David Burch, had written us. I read his short message, then handed it to Brad. With a hopeful smile, Brad told me to get the camera. This was a moment to get on film.

"It's been a hell of a day," I said with joyous exhaustion. "In fact, it's been absolutely brutal." The boat was going a consistent five-and-a-half knots—rocket-ship speed for an ocean rowboat. The waves of anger, sadness, and now joy seemed too dramatic to be real, but David was not one to exaggerate. I read his message out loud: "We're in the Gulf Stream!"

Burch, in a follow-up email, declared it "some sort of miracle."

Opposite: *The first of many counts of our food stores*

PART THREE

—∿∿—

Chapter 10

All about Recovery

When the sea is calm, every ship has a good captain.
—Swedish proverb

The mood changed to a celebratory one. England seemed a week away, maybe two. But we decided to keep meals conspicuously small until a food inventory, which would have to wait until we were well within the major flow of the Gulf Stream. One to two hours of delay on the edge of the current and it could shift from our grasp.

Three options are available for travel by boat from the northeastern seaboard to England: the Great Circle, the Rhumb Line, or the Gulf Stream routes. Unlike the Gulf Stream, the Great Circle and Rhumb Line courses are not exclusive to the North Atlantic. On a Mercator map, with the world made flat, it is possible to draw a line of constant bearing across all meridians (what appears as a straight line) from New York to London. This Rhumb Line manages to avoid all other bits of land. To understand the Great Circle route, put a string on a globe with one end in London and one in New York, and the shortest length of string goes over Newfoundland on its way to London.

Benjamin Franklin is credited with explaining the existence of the Gulf Stream to the world at large, although it has been observed since the first European ships began sailing to the new world. As postmaster general of the American colonies, Franklin knew that merchant ships from London were arriving in Newport, Rhode Island, weeks faster than the swift packet ships (mail ships) that traveled from two hundred miles farther west, from Falmouth (incidentally our intended destination) to New York. Curious how slower ships on a longer route could arrive faster than the sleek packets, Franklin applied his intellect as well as his network of personal contacts. His cousin, a Nantucket whaling captain, informed him that whalers had known about the huge current running up the coast and then northeast for years. In a letter labeled "Sundry Maritime Observations," Franklin relates his cousin's knowledge of the current, explaining that whales liked to feed on its edges and the whalers crossed it regularly, sometimes running into the packet ships sailing into the current. Whale men like his cousin were known to advise the British of the current but found them "too wise to be counseled by simple American fishermen." Franklin performed his own experiments over three North Atlantic crossings before publishing a report. His findings and the incredibly accurate map of the current, based on his cousin's sketches, were ignored by the British. In the midst of the American Revolution, Franklin distributed them to America's French allies. Today even the British acknowledge the Gulf Stream's existence, and steel ships of commerce still consider how the current will affect their course.

The Gulf Stream is about thirty to fifty miles wide, with enormous eddies that can move equally fast in the opposite direction. Because its exact location constantly changes, it was tough to say if following it in the first place was a good strategy in our slow-moving boat. After counsel with David Burch the night before the race, we had decided to commit to the Gulf Stream. It seemed like the best gamble for trying to break the fifty-five-day record. Our opponents had all committed to the significantly shorter Great Circle route. We had outpaced them in New York harbor, and over the course of the next seventeen days we had gained and then lost a hundred-mile lead searching for the current. Now we would see if our strategy would pay off.

—◦◦◦—

Rowing was easy, and in the ripping current I thought of the hurricane-force winds, house-sized waves, and lightning strikes that had not stopped us. Our success now rested on the calculation of calories stored under the deck rather than on figuring out navigation details or surviving inclement weather. This change reminded me of some disturbingly prophetic advice I'd received. On the day the rest of the crew was packing food, I worked alone on the boat in Ballard, finishing odds and ends a week before we shoved off for New York.

At the end of the day I savored the chance to eat, alone, at a local watering hole.

I ordered a gin and tonic. Swigging it down, I ordered another. The regular next to me had a gruff voice and graying brown facial hair. After a few vague answers to his inquiries about what I did, I felt too impolite not to elaborate. He listened quietly and asked a few pointed questions that suggested familiarity with the sea. Sipping his drink, he contemplated the bottles behind the bar. After a few silent moments, with great enunciation, he spoke. "I'll tell you one thing. It's all about how you recover from your first big fuckup."

Day 18

Late afternoon sunlight sparkled on the water. Now deep in the Gulf Stream, we began tackling the food inventory. Hopes were high that it was not as bad as it appeared. The three knots of current taking us in the right direction had made the task easier to digest. Greg was in the cabin, ready to tally items in the yellow waterproof logbook. Brad sat on deck next to the cabin, filming the inventory. He had relinquished control of the food; he was here to explain what he knew and had voluntarily taken himself out of any voting equation should one arise.

Dylan and I unscrewed the ten circular hatches that opened into their own independent, watertight lockers. Each contained enough food to fill half the deck when spread out. The provisions had been separated into breakfasts, dinners, and "snack packs"— random bits of food that would suffice in between each of our six 120-minute rowing shifts per day, including the only stash of candy bars on the boat.

The hatches revealed well-organized foodstuffs—each meal in its own shrink-wrapped bag. A typical meal came with four bags of polenta, four Mylar bags of tuna, some nuts, and a few candy bars. Breakfasts were much the same with more granola, oatmeal, grits, protein milk powder, and candied fruit snacks. Snack packs, which had to meet the requirements of more than one meal, were twice as big. As we counted each hatch, the number of snack packs diminished. The breakfast bags were becoming rarer as well.

Race requirements demanded we take one hundred days' worth of food. Keen to save weight, we agreed to take seventy days of full rations (five thousand to six thousand calories each) and thirty days of half rations, under the assumption that seventy days would be the outer limit of our journey. Woodvale did not initially sign off on our food, and at that point Brad assured us that he could make up the extra with bulk foods and some meals offered by the crew of the *Commando Joe*, who'd brought extra (although Brad did not take all they offered). The random stacks of food piled on the dock looked like enough food for Woodvale to ultimately give an exasperated okay. Whether this was actually what we needed to sustain us was a different story.

Brad's apparent method had broken down; rather than orderly meals some of what we had was completely random food and dry stores. After seventeen days on the water, there were fewer than forty left of each meal and only eleven full-sized snack packs. The rest was mix-matched, including a ten-pound bag of peanuts, two huge bags of granola and unflavored oatmeal, fifty-three Mylar bags of tuna, two massive sacks of dehydrated milk (some of which was already going moldy), some fig bars, crackers, six sausage logs, Gatorade, ground coffee, some dehydrated camp meals, and dissolvable vitamins, these last two items provided at the last minute by my parents. The variety the camp meals promised—from Santa Fe chicken to spaghetti Bolognese—was so precious that we did not even include them in our ration count. Instead, we dubbed them special "thousand-mile meals." Close enough to a thousand miles and depressed after counting food, we decided we had earned a treat that evening.

The last hatch was filled with more than a hundred mysterious camp meals. Each green bag had the same picture of a ginger-haired woman in Daisy Dukes next to a broad-shouldered man sporting a wavy brown mane of hair and a pink flannel shirt, cooking in front of their tent. He was a dead ringer for Baywatch star David Hasselhoff, and for the rest of the trip these were referred to as "Hasselhoffs." With names like "Mum's Apple Pie," it was clear on which side of the Atlantic these meals had originated. These were *Commando Joe*'s extra Hasselhoffs. When packing the boat with food, Brad's logic had been that when the hatch was full, we would be too—a reasonable conclusion considering how low the boat had sat in the water at Liberty Landing Marina. Unfortunately, Brad had counted the Hasselhoffs as a full meal. They contained a measly 250 to 300 calories a pop—about half the calories of a normal-sized American dehydrated camp meal.

My favorite random food item pulled out of the bowels of the boat during the inventory was six days' worth of rice labeled "diarrhea rice" by Greg's mother. In case any of us were in need of the binding qualities of the grain, she had offered this homeopathic remedy. Considering our staples of cheese, polenta, and butter, we would not have this problem. Our primary source of fuel was the 250 pounds of calorie-dense cheese and butter lodged in the bow. This larder was the only food issue I remember discussing with Brad in detail before the trip. Research has revealed that a gram of carbohydrates and protein have roughly the same caloric energy, while fat has roughly twice as many calories for the same weight.

Knowing weight loss was going to be a part of this trip, we had gained a good fifteen pounds each in preparation. Despite the joy I had at eating with utter abandon, my primary concern about our high-fat diet was whether I would be doing any permanent damage to my arteries. After a checkup with a doctor, I was assured that at the rate I would be losing weight, the fat would have no time to stay with me. Fat burns at a slow rate, making it a perfect food for endurance. Consider the countless references to "fatty meat" equating to "good meat" in Lewis and Clark's westward journey. The blubbery seal diet of Captain Ernest Shackleton's *Endurance* crew contributed to their survival during nearly six hundred days spent below the Antarctic Circle.

Humans' use of fat essentially comes from our Neolithic days, when we used it to store energy for inevitable famine. The body stores the fat easily because deep down it still thinks the next meal will only come after another long day's hunting or gathering. The hundreds of pounds of flab in the rowboat's bow was our caloric ace in the hole. Before loading, each pound had been shrink-wrapped and frozen at ten below to aid in preservation. Despite this, and in conjunction with the surprising heat of the North Atlantic summer, the cheese had begun to grow impressive colonies of mold.

Dylan slashed into the bags of several chunks of very fuzzy cheeses and hurled them overboard. Brad and I watched, our silence indicating tacit approval. Arguments existed on each side. Cheese represented a respectable one-twelfth of the boat's weight, and a considerable portion was going bad. Even before the current crisis, Dylan and Greg had long considered this amount of cheese an unwanted anchor. Now that some of it was moldy, they had a justifiable reason to finally send it to sleep with the fish. They dumped between ten and twenty pounds of cheese—an entire two days' worth of calories for the four of us.

I was uneasy. It just seemed like getting rid of any food—in any state—was to tempt fate. After all, cheese is one of the few foods salvageable from mold. I could not bring myself to throw any of it in the water, and kept some of the higher-quality pepper jack for my meal that night after hacking off a thick chunk of mold. Dylan chastised me about it, and I was disturbed that I should have to defend my use of what he was planning to throw overboard.

—⁓—

After the food inventory was complete, optimism ruled the day. It seemed like we had enough food, considering our progress since reaching the Gulf Stream. If we remained in the current at that speed, we would make the halfway point of the North Atlantic in about a week—a mere twenty-four days from starting. If we extrapolated from that pace, we would have thirty-one days left to match the fifty-five-day speed record across the pond.

Brad rowing in the stern with following waves

—⌇⌇—

Chapter 11

Rowing the Ocean
Is Not Enough

The OAR Northwest mantra—the safest crossing is the fastest crossing—touched on five goals we set out from the beginning:

1. Get across alive and uninjured. Less time on the water equates to less time for things to go wrong.
2. Come out of it debt-free; a fast crossing is more marketable and will attract more people.
3. Beat the indomitable Norwegian clamdiggers' fifty-five-day record, or barring that, the four-man Dutch crew's record of sixty days set the year before.
4. Become the first Americans to row the North Atlantic (as defined by the Ocean Rowing Society).
5. Become the first rowboat to cross from mainland United States to mainland United Kingdom without assistance.

Some rowing history is in order. Most ocean rowers have at least contemplated the story of Norwegians George Harbo and Frank Samuelsen, the first people to ever row an ocean. In 1896, in an eighteen-foot open dory boat, they crossed the North Atlantic from Battery Park in Manhattan to the Isles of Scilly off Cornwall—in fifty-five days! This record remained untouched on our race start day, and we wanted it. The record-setting year, 1896, was the height of the Victorian epoch. The Statue of Liberty was starting to show a patina. Fiberglass cloth, now the primary material of our boat, had recently made its debut in a dress three years earlier at the Chicago World Exposition. No explorer had yet made it to the Poles, and vast tracts of the globe remained unknown swaths on maps.

103

Harbo and Samuelsen moved to New York City amid headlines proclaiming discovery and accomplishment. Within easy view of the most modern city in the world, they made their living digging clams on the Hudson River estuary by rowboat. Both men had grown up on the fjords of Scandinavia and had crossed the ocean many times. They understood the sea.

History says it was George's idea, but the duo's motivation was likely a combination of things. The U.S. economy was in a depression in the 1890s. This modern era of possibility had made some men wealthy from the lecture circuit. George, thinking speaking might be an easier job than digging clams, believed there might be room for two Norwegian rowers on the circuit. The two men set about creating the first boat built expressly to row the ocean. It took a year to build and provision the double-ended eighteen-foot lapstrake craft. Lapstrake planking refers to a method of attaching planks to the frames and to other planks in which they lap one edge over another. This method, used for hundreds of years and sometimes referred to as "clinker-built," adds strength to the hull.

The craft was a bit like their clam boat and a bit like the sturdy fishing dories taken on the decks of schooners out to the Grand Banks, with a few extras. Airtight compartments built out of tin helped keep the necessary equipment dry and served as extra buoyancy. Unlike modern ocean rowboats, Harbo and Samuelsen's was not self-righting. To cope with this, handles were built on the outside of the hull. When "turtled," they would use the handles to lever their body weight into position to right the boat before climbing aboard and bailing. Hemp rope was used for lifelines, wax-impregnated canvas for foul-weather gear. Their life vests were stuffed with reindeer hair, chosen because each fiber was hollow and would not eventually soak up water like cork life jackets. For 1896, it was top-of-the-line gear.

Among their many provisions, they carried seventeen bottles of wine, five hundred raw eggs, and a small gas stove for cooking up coffee. There was no EPIRB, VHF, or water maker—and little room for error. Harbo and Samuelsen set out on June 6, keenly aware of the calculated risk. Fifty-five days of Herculean effort brought them to the Scilly archipelago off Cornwall. After a brief stop on shore and a good night's sleep, they rowed on to Le Havre, France, arriving five days later.

I wish I could say this accomplishment became a gold mine for these modest, laconic, Lutheran men, but the lecture circuit was not a natural place for them. News of their feat was well-received when telegraphed from the Isles of Scilly to New York, but it was not important enough to warrant a ticker-tape parade. There was no fanfare when they returned, this time via steamship—just two of many accented immigrants in New York. The feat faded into obscurity. Not much is left in the record to reveal how Harbo and Samuelsen thought of their trip, and their logbook's economy of words provides few clues. Harbo's life was cut short by pneumonia in 1909; he is buried in Brooklyn. Later that same year, Samuelsen moved back to Norway, where he died in 1946. He is buried in the seaside village of Farsund.

—⁓—

Seventy years later, when the two British men, Blyth and Ridgeway, rowed from Cape Cod to the coast of Ireland in ninety-two days, they brought rowing oceans out from complete obscurity to the actual fringes of adventure. In the fifty years since then, many people have rowed the other parts of the Atlantic in fewer than fifty-five days, claiming to beat Harbo and Samuelsen. The routes these claims have taken range from the Canary Islands to the Caribbean, as well as various parts of Newfoundland to parts of Europe. For the sake of comparison, the straight-line distance between New York and the Isles of Scilly is roughly 3250 statute miles. The distance from Tenerife, Canary Islands, to Antigua is just fewer than three thousand statute miles. The distance from St. Johns, Newfoundland, to Falmouth is approximately 2140 statute miles. Each route has its own unique wind and current that affect the average time it takes to make the crossing. Comparing different starting and ending points, even if it is on the same ocean, is comparing apples to oranges.

Another factor to take into account when comparing each record is whether the boat made it to a predetermined line of longitude or made it to shore under its own power. Many ocean rows are completed to a line of longitude and then towed to shore. It is easier to intersect a line of longitude because it extends from the North Pole to the South Pole. A specific location is harder to attain because it usually involves land, and land is subject to strong localized tides and currents. This can make it hard to get to shore in an underpowered vessel.

If we made it to the finish line, we would become the 321st through the 324th people to row an ocean, compared with the 442 who had been launched into space by the end of that summer. Ocean rowing is an obscure sport, both expensive and logistically difficult. It is loosely organized, with a lot of records and various ways to quantify each row. Representing each row in the most flattering light is important. Some of this is ego, but in large part most ocean rowers attempt the feat with the obligation and responsibility to bring back an exceptional result to justify the money spent putting them out there. Greg, Dylan, Brad, and I were as guilty as anyone else in our desire to bring back extras; rowing the ocean was not enough. We wanted to cross faster than fifty-five days because it made good press, and that would be good for our bottom line, considering we did not have enough money to ship the boat back from England. Even if we did beat the record, it would be asinine to compare ourselves to a boat that had two fewer people to row it. But we did anyway.

The Ocean Rowing Society (ORS)—the body that keeps track of records in the sport—distinguishes between modern and historic ocean rows. All rows before 1982 are classed as "historic" because water makers and EPIRBs have fundamentally lowered the level of risk. I would push the definition back further. Any boat rowed after World War II would be aware that airplanes could fly search patterns and rescue boats could use radar and radio. ORS counts ocean rowers from the country of their birth, so Harbo and Samuelsen, despite having immigrated to America, count as Norwegians, and not Americans. Thus we could associate ourselves with the Harbo and Samuelsen tradition and also claim to be the first Americans. Our decision to sell and see ourselves in this way was, from our nascent understanding of marketing, smart and effective. Still, I truly admired the clamdiggers. I had no such qualms about the four-man, sixty-day Dutch record to the line of longitude at Bishop Rock.

Records aside, the food scare had sobered us a great deal. Although it appeared that the situation was not as dire as we had initially thought, it put our goals into perspective. Our mantra—the safest crossing is the fastest crossing—now had real weight.

—\/\/\—

Chapter 12

Ride It Like You Stole It

*How inappropriate to call this planet Earth
when it is quite clearly Ocean.*
—Arthur C. Clarke

Day 21

Behind our heavily polarized sunglasses, the noonday sun remained painfully bright. The water was so smooth it looked like a giant piece of blue silk gently flapped by ten thousand people beyond the horizon. We baked, soaking our long-sleeved sun shirts in the ocean several times a shift. Patterns of powdery-white salt appeared where the water evaporated, leaving the tan fabric starchy stiff. I spent the day in this aquatic Sahara dreaming about the evening shifts— warm enough to row unencumbered by chafing clothes underneath a clear sky filled with a billion pinholes of light.

It was a fitting stage to enjoy Mozart and Tchaikovsky—a pleasure we relished. Unfortunately, the scratchiness coming though the speakers told us that the next round of wet weather would kill them, leaving us to share an iPod.

Even the birds, a near constant presence at sea, seemed to have found some cool place to rest. Days went by without a sighting of any fish or mammal worth noting. A tranquil ocean is a quiet place, and the industry of rowing seemed garishly loud.

The few days after taking the food inventory were mind-numbingly boring and mercifully drama-free. Tall snow-white clouds stood sentinel on the horizon, indicating we were well within the Gulf Stream's boundaries. Between our observations at sea and David Burch's thermal imaging maps, we had concluded that these clouds follow the warm water and thus the current. In the days

There's nothing quite like cooking in the nude with an open flame.

preceding our arrival, these same clouds appeared like a distant mountain pass barring our entry. Now within their borders, we eyed them warily for signs of change to keep the current from sneaking out from under us.

One break in the monotony was cause for celebration. My stepfather had contacted a Pacific Northwest shipping company about flying our boat back to Seattle after the race. This represented one of the last big chunks of unfinished business. To get the ball rolling, they would need a comprehensive list of gear on the boat, which was easy to provide via email. We were grateful for the work Jim had gone to for me and the generosity of these companies.

It was astonishing that all of this could be communicated first-hand, over a thousand miles at sea. Mundane paperwork was not the first thing I thought of when I decided to row the ocean, and I found its existence—really, its necessity—on our tiny vessel fascinatingly frustrating. We did not have to wait like Harbo and Samuelsen to wave our arms at a passing ship and yell that we were all right, then pray the message would be delivered weeks later. Instead, anyone with internet access could send us a text message, and they did—dozens at a time. We were absolutely thrilled by these 120-character snippets of goodwill, but they also fundamentally changed our interaction with the sea.

Each text message silently reminded us to maintain a regular blog. Our ability to communicate from the middle of the ocean became so routine that we were considered negligent when we did not send daily messages into the ether.

The boys and I had discussed on shore what our "responsibility to land" would be at sea. Reading other ocean-rowing blogs in the summer before our trip helped us form some guidelines. After a stern order framed as a request from Dave Spooner, Greg's father, we decided that our blog would not discuss the expected body troubles like butt rashes or boils. We would keep it family-friendly, focusing on the extraordinary, the informative, the fun, the good, and our gratefulness for the opportunity.

To talk about our food issue would have been to bleed in public. Getting something so important so wrong was a loss of face. It would be showing ourselves to be irresponsible and therefore unworthy of the faith people and organizations had put in us and expressed with their money—not to mention how this revelation would worry our long-suffering loved ones. If we kept the truth in the boat, we remained the only people who suffered. With this decision made, each blog post and email was sent with the knowledge of what we had chosen not to write. Thus a few pounds of electronics now saddled us with the responsibility of choosing what our audience should see. We had been doing this anyway, but hiding what was now a critical part of our journey felt very different from editing out the odd butt boil.

Technology made us safer than adventurers before us, and with it came the loss of introspection inherent in absolute isolation. Its mere existence was a tether that kept a part of our minds from fully letting go of land. I wondered what we were missing. But without technology, we could not know, almost in real time, the dozens of details from loved ones and complete strangers that had become a vital morale booster. Our reliance on communication and the expectation to communicate was troubling. This was the ocean, and our vessel a tiny rowboat. Already the saltwater environment had begun to tarnish and corrode the copper connectors of the satellite phone, reminding us that this invisible link to shore was as tenuous as the calm weather.

———

That afternoon Brad asked for some time between shifts to film something important to him. He handed Greg the camera with instructions to shoot. "The occasion here is putting up a decal," he said. "My Aunt Penny died of lung cancer, as did my grandmother. It seemed fitting to have a little tribute to them." Brad had been private about his family, making no effort to talk about his personal experience with lung-related ailments as part of the team's connection with our sponsor ALAW. This was the first time I'd heard his story about Penny and Mum in any detail. These women had meant a lot to him. In the craziness of that day on the dock, the decal in their honor had not made it on the boat.

"We will put the actual decal on with my uncle so that we can have a nice little moment." Brad's stoic solemnity was a sharp contrast to the emotions I wore on my sleeve. Clearly he was disappointed, but unlike the food shortage, this was a mistake Brad could fix. Greg and I watched him create a silver-and-white duct tape frame, which he stuck on the aft cabin. On this he wrote with a black permanent marker in thick neat letters: "In Memory of Penny and Mum." Greg teased him gently about the adhesive qualities of the duct tape, and Brad joked back. We would keep on taping it till it stuck.

―――

Shortly after we resumed rowing, a coal-colored mass surfaced with the smooth undulation of living flesh, breaking the silence with a hiss from its blow hole ten yards from our craft. Greg logged his estimate at forty-five feet or more; it was at the very least as long as our boat—enough to flip or crush us at its will, or even just by accident. Based on the color and shape we glimpsed, the whale could have been a right, sperm, or fin whale. The smallest of these can grow to fifty-five feet, the largest can grow to eighty-eight. If Greg's estimate was correct, this colossus was a small adult or a juvenile. It's hard to comprehend that men hunted these animals in rowboats about the size of ours.

We scanned the horizon for another appearance. Greg joked that it probably had not heard oars in a while. He might not have been too far off. Whales are long-lived mammals; some larger whales live longer than humans. It was entirely possible that our whale could have encountered the thousands of dories rowing out from their schooners to hunt cod in these waters up until the early 1920s. Could the sound of oars touch a distant memory? The world beneath the sea has never been a quiet place, but for creatures like this, the twentieth century drastically changed the amount and type of underwater noise. Larger baleen whales of the type we had just seen have the ability to produce a low-frequency noise that could at one time communicate over thousands of miles. Global shipping's shift from sails to engines has created low-frequency noise pollution compromising this extraordinary ability. As shipping increases, the effect on the whale's communication is akin to having a conversation across a busy highway. The whale, so close but a world apart, did not reappear.

―――

Especially critical for morale and sanity, two weekly events dominated our calendar—one wholesome and one...less so. Starting with Thursday dinner prep, a regular topic was just how each of us would prepare Friday's gumbo ration, our favorite meal. Soupy or thick? Would the butter be added while it was cooking, or after? The other weekly event was made possible by a gift (several gifts, really) from one of the girlfriends. Individually wrapped discreetly in newspaper and stacked in a plastic bag, the pile of nudie magazines weighed nearly four pounds. We cracked open a new magazine on Saturdays, and anticipation never waned.

But by far the largest treat we gave ourselves was a one-off event, a Day 21 gift from the crew at Flying Spot Entertainment. With a wink and a giggle, Todd and Kathy had handed over this package three weeks ago, and it had promptly been stashed in the bow. On this auspicious day, as the sun began its descent, we were eager to take a break from productive activity. We even put on pants to film the occasion. As captain, I had the honor of opening the gift.

The first object was a large white cotton sheet, which elicited a hearty laugh. Not a lot of privacy exists on a twenty-nine-foot boat, and for us to stay sane we'd agreed that some amount of alone time must be carved out. Dubbed "white sheet time," this activity deserved its own protocol. During the daytime, if the weather was fair and no important task loomed, it was acceptable to ask one's rowing mate in advance for "white sheet time." With some fabric hastily stretched over the hatch, the other rower would stay on deck and cook or make coffee, while for a few private moments one could pretend to be master of his own domain. Todd and Kathy thought the protocol was hilarious—and practical. An actual white sheet had not been part of our supplies; we'd been improvising with a blue camp towel. The white sheet was blessedly clean, and the cotton felt luxurious on my salty skin. I wrapped it around my shoulders toga-style, giving our Day 21 fest a fraternity-party vibe.

The package also included a sack of premium albacore tuna, a card with some inspirational notes from the Flying Spot staff, and four tiny bottles of booze. The scent of the sun-warmed whisky itself was intoxicating. Floating gently in the last of the sun's heat, we sipped our booze and joked easily with each other, telling stories of not-so-distant glory days from college. For a moment the entire boat relaxed.

Day 22

We were about one hundred miles from the halfway point between New York and Falmouth. From here, if we kept an average speed of 2.1 knots (roughly 2.5 miles per hour), we would make it in fifty-five days. Our sprint aided by the Gulf Stream was nearly over, as our required heading angled north. It had been a depressingly short time considering the grief that reaching it had caused, yet after nearly four days since our ration count, the eighty miles per day had begun to add up.

The coordinates for the finish line began at Bishop Rock and ran south along its line of longitude for fifty miles. Bishop Rock is part of the 140-island archipelago twenty-eight nautical miles off the coast of England known as the Isles of Scilly. This small, relatively unknown set of islands is home to just over two thousand. Like many hard-to-reach places, these islands have remained relatively unspoiled, and ecotourism has replaced the more colorful industries of fishing, piloting, and smuggling from days gone by. In medieval times this tiny rock outcropping on the west of England was used as a place of execution; the unlucky were left to die of exposure. In 1858 a lighthouse was built. It was the world's smallest inhabited island until 1992, when the iconic Bishop Rock Lighthouse became fully automated. It is most popularly known as the accepted start and finish point for any vessel's North Atlantic crossing.

Our invisible fifty-mile-long "finish line" seemed generous, but it was short when compared with the length of the race. Following the Gulf Stream east would put us too far south of the finish line and, although we could make greater speed in that direction, it would eventually take us past the fifty-mile-long finish gate in its entirety or make us fight our way north to try and reach it. Watching our competitors cross the finish while we backtracked was not in our race plan.

—◆—

Twenty to thirty dolphins appeared that afternoon. Greg carved out a bait-sized chunk of his knee on a hatch scrambling for the perfect shot, as they flung themselves in tandem out of the water like a choreographed show at Sea World. The animal activity seemed to motivate us to do many of the chores we had neglected. Dylan washed his clothes, putting his spandex, long underwear, and socks in a large five-gallon plastic bag filled with saltwater and a liberal splash of dish soap. To everyone's horror, the bag turned brown—odd considering that the last bits of earth on our deck that had been trod onto the boat by people's feet had long washed off. This filthy cocktail was the creation of our own bodies in a world without dirt. It took four soaks to rinse all the dirty brown water out of his attire. Washing would become a more regular activity from now on.

The past three weeks of rowing varied from hard to very, very hard. We blissfully assumed that because there was no Gulf Stream to follow in the second half, the North Atlantic would be somehow less volatile and more predictable. Crossing the halfway point in under a month had become cause for celebration, and our families made a rapid scramble to change airline tickets to plan for a much earlier arrival in Falmouth. It was as if we had all entered a delusional state and imagined that the ocean adhered to the same laws as solid ground.

Chapter 13

From Here to Eternity

Day 23

Waves glowed as a billion plump raindrops collided with the water and vaporized into a low, gray mist. From this turbulence, a familiar pungent odor emerged. Weeks ago I had realized the smells I had associated with the ocean disappeared away from the shore. My initial theory was that our immersion into this world had made us unable to detect the smell anymore. But I discovered that the odor I called "the ocean" my entire life was actually the seashore, the convergence of water and earth that remains an environment all its own. Tides expose a seabed full of creatures and plants both dead and alive; as the tireless bacteria eat them, they create the waste gas associated with the smell of the sea. Breaking waves constantly tumble and oxygenate the water into an easy-to-smell vapor. Now the smashing onslaught of monsoonlike rain unlocked similar smells of the pelagic plants and animals below the surface.

Dylan and I rowed from dusk into evening, each stroke in the successive waves light and rewarding. Our deck was finally clean as we enjoyed a tiny rainstorm that encompassed our world. This petite deluge was one of many plainly visible to us in the distance as dark gray trapezoids full of water, striding between heaven and sea. The yellow-and-pink sun falling into the ocean reflected light between the surface of the water and the bottom of the pouring clouds, filling each raindrop with color. For the first time since leaving New York, the wind and the waves coincided in our favor, and we welcomed the

Brad and Greg row—shortly after we found out about the food.

chance to surf. Each roll of churning water approaching the stern was sized up by the stroke seat, leading both of us in building up speed on the face of the wave with one, two, or three vigorous swings of the oar. As the water overwhelmed the rear cabin, there would be a perceptible drop in momentum as it rolled by, filling the deck through the scuppers. As the back of the wave reached the bow, the surface tension held the boat in a surging pull forward with a rush of water.

Greg's parents had optimistically planned our landing on August 2, or Day 54—thirty-one days from now. If the weather held, this arrival seemed a real possibility.

—*≈*—

Dylan had begun having "I-want-to-be-on-land days." He summed up the feeling like this: "It's the same frustration you would have with any of your coworkers, except you have to live with them in a tent and work overtime without pay." As long as Dylan could occasionally declare that "Brad's being a bitch," "Greg's a pompous ass," and "Jordan's a slob," he always returned to his Zen mountaintop. Perhaps this poise stemmed from the genetic gift of a sturdy body that seemed perfectly built for hard labor in awful conditions. At five foot ten he was the shortest of us by nearly five inches, and his large barrel chest was perched on proportionally sturdy legs. As we all had, Dylan let his weight rise up to 220 pounds before leaving New York. As the weight peeled off of us revealing ribs, he remained a picture of health. While we cowered in sun shirts that kept our pasty skin safe from blistering, Dylan basked in its rays, turning a healthy Mediterranean brown. Even his facial hair grew in moderation. As the rest of us hurtled toward castaway couture, he looked like he had spent a rejuvenating week in the woods.

Brad and Greg were nearing the end of their first shift together since the food confession, and they remained quiet. Fortunately, the tandem concentration required while surfing was a good excuse for minimal talk. Had their shift begun in the midst of the tedious flat water, the absence of idle chitchat over four days would have made for a very loud silence. Brad had been eager to row with Greg, hoping to rebuild a bridge of trust but not knowing if it could be done. Greg's anger and disappointment had appeared to die down and their interactions had become civil, both men doggedly determined that their working relationship would not break.

———✸———

The Fourth of July dawned. Wind fanned the electric blue water like flames over wood. Waves leapt into our aft hatch, forcing us to shut it, putting an end to the glorious cross breeze that ventilated and dried the sweltering cabin. We were making our last move within the borderland of the Gulf Stream; soon we would turn slightly north and say good-bye to the keystone of our cross-Atlantic strategy.

Like eager children on the streets of Anytown, USA, we could not be convinced to wait until dark to start our fireworks show. We decided that one nonemergency flare should be requisitioned for celebration. It was Greg's favorite holiday and the first day he felt slightly homesick. Were he on land, he would have been at his childhood home on Bainbridge Island, where he had been with the same friends, at the same parade, for most of his life. A seventy-dollar firework seemed a small price for a nod at tradition.

With a mischievous grin, Brad pulled the flare out of its dry bag. "I'm feeling patriotic now that I got something I can explode." I understood the feeling, and felt something like Greg's homesickness. I wondered if my younger brother, Douglas, would succeed in his annual mission to ignite my parents' neighborhood in New Mexico.

Brad studied the instructions, held it away from his face, and pulled the tab. The rocket illuminated the deck as the tiny ascending meteor headed toward its apex a thousand feet above us, visible for fifty miles. The payload burned white and drifted down to earth much like the model rockets Jim Wood had introduced me to as a child. We gazed, transfixed at the floating light, thrilled at the acrid smell of gunpowder. Dylan began singing "Happy Birthday" to America, and we all joined in, our voices drunk with joy. There was not a more enthusiastic rendition sung a thousand miles in either direction. It was good, on our nation's birthday, to be ahead of the likable redcoats we had so briefly known in New York. It would have felt much different to be losing to them on this day. In seconds the party was over. It was, as Dylan succinctly put it, time to "kick some British ass."

—◠◠◠—

Light rain greeted Dylan and me on our first full evening shift. In minutes it opened up into a biblical deluge. Had it been cold, I would have thought the raindrops were volleys of hail. The air, full of falling water, created an unholy dark, broken only by lightning searing our corneas into temporary blindness. The bright orange screens of our navigation instrumentation glowed unnaturally on the bulkhead. Bioluminescence activated by the downpour looked like the reflection of stars on a rapidly evolving Milky Way. Sweet, freshwater bypassed our hoods, pouring onto our faces and into our mouths as if we were rowing through the faucet that fed the ocean. Minutes before our shift was over, the abuse ended as suddenly as it appeared. Brad and Greg slept through it all. The world they woke up to was merely a cloudy, slightly windy morning. Dylan and I retreated to the cabin giggling maniacally before collapsing into sleep.

Day 26

Shift change. I switched to rowing with Brad again. Waves had no particular direction, and the current seemed to shift constantly. We suspected that we remained on the edge of the Gulf Stream, and that the conditions would level out as we increased our distance from it. Cold and damp weather would be with us for a while. That night, Dylan and Greg found it difficult to stay awake on the oars. They paused and ate a precious candy bar for some quick energy. Even with our reduced rations of one bar per rower every forty-eight hours, they would not last long. Blood sugar fortified, they had returned to rowing by touch in the cloud-covered night when a broad swath of water below the boat began to glow. This was another whale, its colossal power evident in its huge gentle movement. Dylan and Greg clipped into their lifelines, but the whale soon passed the boat.

Brad and I stepped out of the cabin to row the next morning as reasonably rested as we could expect. Hunger had begun to eat at me, and I was not feeling as forgiving as I had at Brad's first confession eight days earlier. Tension had begun to surface, and we bitched like an unpleasant old married couple. A half hour into our shift, a cold front moved in from the north, bringing low clouds and a twenty-degree drop in temperature. I have never experienced a faster change in weather. Wind and current were at odds. Despite knowing our location on the GPS to 0.01 degree, it felt as if we were suddenly lost. The open domain of the ocean had closed and we found ourselves in an inescapable, invisible cage. In twenty-four hours our speed had dropped from a brisk 4 knots to 1.5 knots (4.7 to 1.7 mph). As the Woodvale weather report put it: "typical North Atlantic rowing conditions."

—~~—

Chapter 14

Cleanliness Is Next to Hungriness

Sleeping, cooking, cleaning, navigating, even brushing our teeth became jobs planned hours in advance. Rowing was the easy part. Of these inglorious chores the fight for personal hygiene would pose our greatest nonemergency threat. No matter how much care was taken, the regular downpours soaked into every nook and cranny of the cabin. Each soaking shift transition ended by latching the hatch against the elements. We'd then remove our spandex or long underwear, and the futile, yet vitally important, crotch-drying campaign carried on.

After nearly a month at sea, it was painfully obvious that next to the health of our hands, the wellness of our derrieres was strategic to success. Our fight had reached an uneasy stalemate. The dreaded "saltwater sores" had not appeared. Instead, ingrown hairs seemed the primary sources of aggravation, caused from sweating in unwashed clothing. The slightest pressure unleashed a sting akin to some malevolent nurse plunging a hypodermic syringe into the offending area. Greg confessed this was the closest he had ever come to crying from physical pain since grade school.

Along with the need for constant airing was consistent washing of both body and clothing, which we had neglected our first week at sea. Problem spots had entrenched themselves and would be with us until England. Nothing more could be done, save washing at minimum every two to three days. Any longer and the outside of our bodies began to hurt. This minimum of self-care maintained the line between simple discomfort and a painful medical problem.

Another third-grade student from West Woodland illustrates an eerily accurate vignette of life at sea after joining the Gulf Stream.

Day 28

July 7 came with the first real break in rain in three days. Each successive morning my belly grew progressively empty by the end of each shift. The fifteen to twenty pounds of extra weight we'd each gained before the trip had given us fifty thousand to seventy thousand extra calories stored in our bodies. Burning a conservative estimate of eight thousand calories a day from the twelve hours behind the oars meant that we started the voyage allegedly carrying about six to nine days of supplemental fuel to burn. After twenty-seven days at sea, all of us were back to our pre-bulked weight. We were very hungry, but not starving. Each day we consumed roughly twenty-four hundred to twenty-eight hundred calories over two main meals. People of modest means outside of industrialized countries work long, full days of manual labor with less food. It was the first time I experienced what it felt like to eat, to still be hungry, and to work through it, just waiting until the next meal.

The question was unavoidable: Would hunger cause us to sacrifice our goal? It wasn't a matter of life or death—surely we would survive on smaller rations of food—but our performance and stamina were at stake. We could surrender our ambition, call Mark Terry and the crew on *Sula*, and ask for supplies. The thought was heartbreaking, but could we really deal with the effects of chronic hunger? The feeling was becoming familiar; my ability to fight impulsive, selfish, and defeatist thoughts was dwindling in this fragile community of four. *Sula* made its second and final visit that morning. Mark and the crew's last visit had proved such a pleasant diversion that now the whole boat buzzed with the anticipation of company. The visit quickly devolved into salvos of good-natured insults. We mentioned nothing about the food—optimistic that we could make the whole expedition without revealing our mistake. The lack of food had not yet begun to show, especially under our loose sun shirts.

Mark identified the new current that was giving us so much trouble as the Azores. It would disappear north of us. Our navigator back home, David Burch, was less convinced of its identity, however; he told us the Azores current was several hundred miles southeast of us. The current at hand, he wrote in the tired tone of a tenured professor, was likely "just a large random patch of bad water, of which there are many scattered over the ocean." Since *Sula* had just come from the north, he urged us to consider their advice, just not to call it the Azores current.

It was gumbo night and everyone was happy for the weekly reward meal, quite ready to forego the usual cheese, tuna, and mashed potatoes or polenta for our evening meal. As expected, the powdered mix took us to Valhalla with culinary delight. But by midnight, the happy memory of gumbo was long gone. Dylan finished his first night shift in constant pain from hunger. He had felt this way for three days, but two hours of sleep and two more hours of rowing stood between him and breakfast. Often the satisfaction of covering any distance over six miles in a shift eased the hurt, but nights like tonight—with fewer than three miles of progress for two hard hours of rowing—gave little satisfaction.

—◦◦◦—

A magnificent yellow sun rose over a sapphire seascape. Luck seemed to change that morning, as waves built from ten to nearly fifteen feet with wind coming directly out of the southwest at twenty-five knots. Not since Tropical Storm Alberto had we rowed waves this large. Good wind was blowing us in the direction we desired. The current still ran against us, steepening the waves into a disorganized mess and turning our earlier massive progress into a slow but respectable 3.2 knots.

Dylan and Greg fought to maintain cadence. Their blades thrust hard into the water to apply what power was possible to its morphing surface. They swayed like punch-drunk boxers, and wind tore the words from their mouths. The gates on the oarlocks now remained open. Each time an unruly wave wrenched it from our hand, the resilient nylon gate would twist and drop the oar instead of snapping the pin. We still had four thole pins left. The operation of dropping the heavy shafts back into the oarlock did require considerable precision and patience, but by now we could do the whole maneuver with one arm without breaking rhythm.

Around two that afternoon, Brad and I woke to a depressing sight. Rain had come and the waves had dropped to five feet. The wind had shifted from the southwest to north-by-northeast.

Our speed had plummeted to less than one knot. Greg and Dylan were only too happy to pass off the gloomy situation. For Dylan, the dismal rowing progress did not matter. He had just called his girlfriend, Emily, on the satellite phone. Glossing over the details of our tribulations, he had emphasized what a good time we were having on the ocean. He was much more eager to hear how she was doing and for a few moments to live vicariously through her. His shoulders began to shudder, and we realized he was crying. His large hands seemed to mime running through her hair. She had sold her car to buy a ticket to England. The whole boat could not have heard better news.

Toward the end of our shift Brad and I simply stopped rowing. It was useless—two frustrating hours to make one mile. Any direction we rowed that could possibly benefit us was closed as wind, waves, and current conspired against us. Someone suggested a hull cleaning, and the depressing conditions evaporated at the prospect of productive work. It was the first time I had left the boat in the open ocean. I jumped in, glad to be attached by a stout lifeline. Looking immediately down with goggles, I saw a progression of the lightest blue to deepest black to land more than two miles below. Brown seaweed and gooseneck barnacles had grown on the outside of the hull. It had been twelve days since Brad's cleaning.

Other than what I removed from the hull, the water seemed uncharacteristically void of life—as if the fickle elements that slowed our progress had also scared away the sea life. It felt good to swim, but I was relieved to be back on deck and moving slowly away from this empty, eerie part of the sea.

Day 29 came bright and fresh, with wind light and favorable out of the west, pushing us toward England. We trudged along at 1.4 knots. The strong, unfavorable current beneath us made each beautiful wave we rolled down a depressing facsimile of progress. Four days of on-again, off-again rain, combined with the morning's hunger pangs, made conversation with Brad impossible for me until I had breakfast. Not usually chatty in the early hours, Brad came out of the cabin chipper and talkative. I grunted one-word answers, staring with growing rage at the back of his head.

Each gnawing pull was grinding out the last of the civility and compassion I had been able to muster since Brad's revelation about the food shortage. The boat began to pick up in speed. "Brad," I finally said, "in the mornings, I just can't talk to you."

He cocked his head. "Okay." The speed cruised up to three then to over four knots.

"Brad?" I asked sharply, grabbing his attention. "I want you to know . . . ," I paused, thinking carefully about what I wanted to say. "Everybody made mistakes on this trip, but you fucked up worse than anybody else." My adrenaline racing as I rowed, I would probably feel the results of this expenditure for the rest of this day and perhaps the next.

Brad sat up straighter, our oars mirroring each other perfectly. "That's not fair," he said, with an icy tone.

A few strokes, just as hard, passed as I considered this. "I know and I don't care."

The boat was flying like it had four weeks ago, as we'd raced for the Verrazano-Narrows Bridge. Each stroke snapped crisply. For several minutes we hauled thousands of pounds of fat, heavy boat through the waves, each of us too proud to stop. In one stroke we realized that our fates were tied. Expending excess energy in these conditions was as stupid as throwing food overboard. We resumed our frustratingly slow and maintainable pace, our breath long and deep, in unbroken quiet for the rest of the two-hour shift.

—⁓—

In the halcyon days of our rowing in the Gulf Stream, going over an average of eighty miles a day, all sins had seemed forgiven—or at least forgotten. Brad had understood that he could not dwell on his failure if he was going to be a productive crewmate. Necessary as this was for his own resilience, it skewed his vision of how the rest of us were handling the austerity measures. I was sorry for my anger, but I could no longer help or hide it. Only during breakfast that day did civility and compassion return. I asked Brad to hand over the camp stove. I said "please," and he said "you're welcome."

The numbers were against us. Had we maintained an average speed of 2.5 knots, it's likely my anger might never have come to a head. Trip-time estimations on land ranged between forty and seventy days—fifteen days on either side of Harbo and Samuelsen's record. As our hourly speed decreased, the overall average velocity we would need to maintain to arrive by fifty-five days increased. Four days earlier, we needed to maintain 2.1 knots, or just over fifty miles a day to break the record. Now we needed 2.5, or sixty miles a day. A tenth of a knot over several weeks added up to days. Even with all of our rationing, we did not have enough food on this boat for seventy days. We were coming to terms with not making the crossing in fifty-five days. Having to consider the possibility of needing to accept food from the race organizers was too much. That would mean disqualification, tantamount to failure. However, there was no fighting it. The sea would let us pass in its own time, and at 1.4 knots we would run out of food.

Brad could row, do extra chores, and pray. That was all he could do on this boat, and it might not be enough. Our judgment over him, fair or not, would be based on the ocean's uncontrollable whims. It was a question of how we defined success. Making it to New York had been a milestone, and getting to England unassisted, setting a record, winning this race—all of that had been part of our definition of success. What had we sacrificed eighteen months of our lives preparing for? What would we still have to sacrifice to succeed? And if we failed, what then?

—◊◊◊—

Dylan was in as good a mood as ever. His girlfriend was coming to England. He was the skinniest he'd ever been. The last four days it had taken to get out of the Gulf Stream were harder than the few weeks it had taken to find it. Dylan had made his own calculations. Brad had brought roughly fifty days of food at five thousand to six thousand calories each. At the start of the trip there had been thirty-five snack packs and just fewer than sixty dinners and breakfasts. The team had agreed on seventy days of full rations followed by thirty days of half rations, so things did not add up.

"That's not a mistake," Dylan said, "it's a lack of something." Resigned to his frustration, he made a point not to complain directly to Brad. In what I thought to be an incredibly forgiving gesture—something I hoped we all had the strength to do—Dylan said he didn't want to ruin Brad's experience. Dylan would not be comfortable until we got to England, but hoped he would be at peace with what happened. "If we win," he concluded, "it's going to be a lot easier to walk away from this."

In a moment of clarity, I had come up with the idea of stretching each two days of dinner packs to three days. This was easy to do with the polenta and dehydrated mashed potatoes, and everyone seemed enthusiastic: this would turn our thirty remaining dinners into forty-five. Half of each night's protein ration, usually a bag of tuna but sometimes chicken or shrimp, would be allotted to snack food. Dylan was optimistic but less enthusiastic about the upcoming "rice week" as we began to dip into the ominously labeled "diarrhea rice" for some variety.

—∿∿—

The evening sun was low enough on the horizon to allow us to look directly into it. Smooth cobalt rollers—the first long and low waves of this kind we experienced on the Atlantic—rushed softly toward the boat, gently lifting and dipping our tiny craft. Like an aquatic yellow brick road, the descending orb lit a glinting path. We watched it slip into an evening gown of green, pink, and gold clouds until it disappeared beneath the blue.

PART FOUR

Once out of the Gulf Stream we had few warm days ahead of us.

Chapter 15

—ᐧᴧᴧᐧ—

Visitation

Day 31

Roughly forty coal-colored bodies up to twenty feet in length surrounded us. Squeaks, whistles, and clicks were audible above the surface. The heads were large and bulbous with broad mouths. Either they had stumbled upon our strange and quiet form of transportation or they had heard and sought us out. Pilot whales had appeared before in groups of three and four, swimming past us without a gesture of acknowledgment. This time was different. They dipped and bobbed above the waves, lazily circling us, some lying like waterlogged driftwood just beneath the surface. Flukes would splash and the occasional glossy black face would glide past us with an onyx eye fixed in observation. Beneath our boat, an amorous pair made baby pilot whales.

The scientific name for this behavior is apt: "loafing." Pilot whales' muscular, bulky bodies balance endurance and sprinting power, diving as deep as three thousand feet to hunt large squid. In the darkness their eyes are useless, so they use sonar clicks to locate their prey. As they approach, these clicks increase up to three hundred per second, creating a pattern of reflected sound that guides them as they sprint toward prey at twenty mph for up to 650 feet. This all-or-nothing style of hunting is the suspected reason for the animal's reputation for docility on the surface. They loaf about and appear friendly because of sheer exhaustion.

Greg and I called quietly into the cabin for Dylan and Brad. We had to get this on film. This was the pilot whales' space; they needed no rock to call home. We had met them on as equal terms as I could imagine, pulling here on muscle power alone. For nearly twenty minutes they played around us, splashing lazily. They broke the spell first and meandered away from our still vessel thinking, no doubt, of their next squid hunt.

—⁓—

That afternoon my mother forwarded me an email from Gerry Gallagher. He and his wife Kim are old family friends from Sligo, Ireland. Gerry had read an article about the trip and of our team's plan to climb Knocknarea, the mountain outside the town where my father's ashes are scattered, after finishing in England. With my blessing, Gerry was going to put me in touch with the editor of the local paper, the *Sligo Champion*, to see if he could arrange a reception with the city's mayor. In 1969, when my family, after more than eighty years of making scales in Chicago, moved to Ireland, their manufacturing plant became one of the primary employers in what was then a very small town on the west coast. It remained so for over twenty years. When it was sold, the factory continued to manufacture scales under the Hanson name until it closed in 2002. Gerry and others in Sligo were moved that I would return to visit my father's resting place.

As people from my father's past came out of the woodwork, I began to see a cosmic plan. The ocean had called for me, and I would be done with this journey only after I discovered what I had come for. In a boat named for my dead father, it seemed like the purpose of my quest should have been obvious to me. I had long thought I had come to terms with his death, which was awful and unfair as any other but did not make me special. Throughout high school and college I'd prided myself on the "adult" way I viewed my father's death—a sad event that did not and would not influence who I was. My faults would be my own. All things considered, I was incredibly lucky. I had a loving family and led a privileged life. I could add up all the good things in my life and weigh them against the scale of the unknown, of what might have been had he not passed, and tell myself with complete honesty that life was good. As much as I had wanted him to live, still missed him, and hated never knowing him, if some alternate universe existed, I would not trade lives with my counterpart who at three had not lost his father.

What would my life have been like with my father? It was an entirely philosophical exercise. At one point in my life I would have traded my own existence to know him as a man; this new conclusion was not easy. Before his death, James Robert Hanssen had provided me with more than genes and love. From travel to college, my inheritance—built on generations of success—had set the trajectory that made this rowing project possible for me. Yet to compare it to twenty years of life with my mother, my stepfather Jim, and Douglas (a result of their union, who at seventeen was becoming an increasingly awesome individual), I no longer had to ask myself that hypothetical question. What-ifs and childhood fantasies of sitting down to talk with my father could wait until my death.

The Hanssens wondered if three was too young to remember. I had never found it difficult to call Jim Wood "Dad"—except in front of my paternal grandparents, uncle, and aunt. As much as I needed a dad—and found one in Jim Wood—I remained the son of their eldest son and brother. They were glad I had a new father, yet as much as he loved me, he was not their son. At six, three years was half a lifetime to me but a fresh wound to parents who had lost a child. I had always sensed this, and the sadness it brought. So I always spoke carefully when around them, awkwardly altering my sentences from "my dad" to "Jim Wood" to make sure they knew whom I was talking about. Each time I exchanged "Jim Wood" for "Dad" in front of them, though, it felt like reverse betrayal. I could find no equitable term, because in my mind both men were my fathers. No one else seemed to entirely understand that. Attaching the prefix "step-" to Jim Wood's fatherhood rang hollow. I was over twenty when I first consciously referred to Jim Wood as my dad in front of my Hanssen grandparents. They had grown to love Jim by then, and treated Douglas exactly as they treated me—as an adored grandson.

Proving by some epic act that I had not and would never forget Jim Hanssen did not consciously cross my mind. I had decided to do this because I wanted to row across the ocean. Honoring his memory had never been the impetus for the plan. Naming the vessel after him made me examine how his death had affected my life. Each two-hour shift I looked at his picture on the bulkhead, having a one-sided conversation that ended with more questions. My actions, although entirely my own choices, were influenced and guided by Jim Hanssen's legacy as much as my day-to-day life with my mother and Jim Wood had been.

How this adventure honored my father perplexed me. I prayed for clarity by the time I got to Ireland.

Avoiding freighters and tankers was a top priority.
This one is about a mile away.

Chapter 16

Irregular Rowing Syndrome

Day 32

A ghostly apparition of a ship sailed out of the fog revealing itself close off our starboard bow. Dylan and Brad immediately changed direction, taking their best guess on what would place us perpendicular to the oncoming ship. They yelled frantically into the cabin for me or Greg to hail the craft on the VHF. "This is ocean rowboat *James Robert Hanssen* hailing oncoming ship to the southeast," Greg said. He awaited a response, then tried again. "You are headed in our direction. We are a rowboat, repeat, a rowboat. Do you copy?"

I could hear Greg's increasing effort not to sound panicked. The course of the ship, dark and wreathed in lights, was still impossible to determine. Then a calm, French-accented voice spoke: "This is tanker ship *Cipola*. We copy you."

"That's great to hear. Did you see us on your radar?" Greg asked.

The nonchalance was startling. "We have you on radar. Do not worry." You could almost hear him flipping through a magazine without gazing out the windows from his heated bridge.

"Do you have visual confirmation of us?" Greg pressed.

There was another long pause. "Yes...we see you." The *Cipola*, "onion" in Italian, was a 633-foot gas tanker bound for New York. The ship passed a quarter mile away, its crane's silhouette spectral in the moonlight. Its rumbling engines reverberated in our chests.

A collision was a threat we took very seriously, but the reality was that the inane tasks of everyday life on the boat were the most likely and imminent threat to progress. That day Greg looked hopelessly dejected. He stood in the footwell wearing nothing but a short-sleeved shirt, a slightly effeminate yellow sun hat, and wraparound sunglasses. For twenty-four hours he had, to my frustration as his rowing partner, taken longer and longer bathroom breaks.

He took a sip of coffee and scowled miserably. "Drinking that cup of coffee is the hardest thing I've ever had to do," he said.

I rolled my eyes. This from a man thirty-two days into rowing across the ocean. In the past eighteen months I had found Greg to be physically strong, brave, resourceful, pragmatic, and hardworking—perhaps even a bit more manly than average. That being said, curious contradictions existed. He could not handle anything too sour, spicy, or hot. When I bought coffee for us back in Seattle—a coffee town if there ever was one—I would order three black coffees and a hot cocoa, cooled down, for Greg. I was once asked by a barista if the cocoa was for my child.

I expected Greg to be a big boy out here on the ocean. As far as I was concerned, his dislike of coffee meant we were less likely to run out of it. However, given his frequent (and unsuccessful) bathroom breaks—and coffee's well-known side effects—we encouraged, coerced, and eventually begged him to drink a pot. That was two days ago. The stubborn Spooner had finally acquiesced.

He looked at me on the oars, his voice suddenly peppy and full of optimism. "I'm about to blitz this thing with everything we have in the medicine cabinet." I nodded in encouragement and watched him line up two packets of Metamucil, a half dozen fiber pills, and what looked like a huge pink plastic dairy creamer labeled Milk of Magnesia next to the liter of coffee. He mixed each packet of Metamucil and downed them enthusiastically until he got to the bottom, where the gelatinous fiber sludge had settled. He opened the Milk of Magnesia, sniffing it cautiously before shooting it down.

"Tastes like chalk," Greg said, casually shrugging. "Still, tastes better than coffee." I shook my head, thinking about what that toxic concoction might do to him. "One, two, three, four hours I'll be flowing. I'll terrorize that bucket," he predicted.

—⁓—

Nothing but Mother Nature had kept us from the oars. Tropical Storm Alberto, lightning, and squalls coming directly from the northeast did have the power to stop us. Exhaustion, late-night hallucinations, vomiting sea sickness, a growing and empty hunger, various scrapes and bruises, epic ingrown hairs and crotch rot—all had slowed us down but none of these trials had kept anyone from rowing. Inglorious constipation would claim that dubious honor.

Eight minutes later, Greg was doubled over on deck, breathing irregularly. I kept rowing. "What's the status?" I asked cautiously.

"Something's happening . . . inside . . . there is some serious fire." Greg was nearly incoherent with pain. He wasn't going to be rowing any time soon. For the first time on the journey we altered our rowing schedule. Down one man, each rower's shift was split into three forty-five-minute segments. The first and last of each shift were rowed by pairs, with one forty-five-minute shift rowed alone.

It was a quiet day as Dylan, Brad, and I rowed along, trying to ignore the proverbial elephant in the room. We tried to give Greg his space between public and private exertions. All the while, the three of us sat awkwardly on deck exchanging worried looks and unavoidable puns, consciously sipping on coffee. That evening Greg ascended the bucket for the third and final time that day. Seventy-two minutes of silence descended upon the vessel. The success of this trip had come down not to ship collisions, sharks, or storms, but to a great big shit. With a final grunt, indistinguishable from the rest of his efforts, Greg won the battle. "It's done," he said quietly.

He had gone the distance. A celebratory mood settled on the boat. Greg did not move for another twenty minutes before solemnly deep-sixing the contents into the sea. He slept for eight hours.

—⁓—

Morning revealed itself in all its glory and Greg resumed rowing, looking gaunt and exhausted. He had eaten less during the past twenty-four hours. All of us had endured some constipation to a limited extent; we were now aware of just how serious it could be. Weather had been kind to us during Greg's ordeal, and we were closing in on the two-thousand-mile mark at a very respectable 2.5 to 3 knots.

David Burch told us of a low-pressure system coming in the next forty-eight hours. The system would start out against us, and then move around behind us with favorable winds. It was no Alberto, but the thought of being constantly wet again began to wear on me. The next shift, Dylan and I were greeted with rain and wind, our extremities instantly cold and clammy. The current was against us.

Back home, our arrival seemed assured to our loved ones. A "halfway party" at the aptly named Atlantic Crossing pub in Seattle had been planned. We posted the invite to our blog and dreamed of stable ground, live music, and cold beer, a dream that made the shift in current all the more depressing. Our speed dropped from three knots to less than one in a matter of hours. Hearing about the party via email emphasized our remoteness.

Each mile gained was one fewer to make up when the storm blew us backward—but at 0.8 knots, it was slow going. We tossed the sea anchor overboard. Minor repairs and another food inventory kept us busy enough to feel like time was well spent. After our chores, Dylan and I bundled up on deck and drank copious amounts of coffee, almost reaching a state of relaxation. We finally altered our shifts to three hours on, three hours off, allowing the two men in the cabin more time to find some real rest. After six hours the weather system shifted around us, and as Burch had promised began blowing us toward England.

Forty-eight hours into the rough weather I had to remind myself that the wind, as long as it blew eastward, was a good thing. Shift after shift irate waves—not huge waves that our vessel rolled over, but medium-sized whitecaps—knocked us off our seats, into oar handles or the gunwales, covering us with tender yellow bruising. Exclamations of concern gave away to cackles of laughter. This "impact rowing" would not kill us, but the state of continuous wetness just might. The hatch remained shut and the inside cabin cold and humid. Comfort was impossible. The dry suits had come out; for all the waves they deflected, our skin seemed to ferment inside them.

Night after night another combination of oarsmen would nod off, physically depleted, until a yell or a wave brought them out of a dark and miserable dream into the dark and miserable reality. I could hardly sleep for fear of the dreaded ten-, five-, and two-minute yells signaling the crew change. With a surge of adrenaline, Dylan and I would wake, taking turns pulling on our dry suits in the artificial cabin light before stepping outside.

Day 38

On the morning of July 17 the clouds broke, exposing bright blue patches. For the first time in thirty-six hours I was somewhat warm and dry. I realized just how miserably cold the past few days had been. But it had been worth it—we had made good time. The lack of food was becoming more of an issue, however. After our latest count, we felt the prudent thing to do was to finally let Burch and the film crew know, with express orders not to tell our families. Brad penned the email: "Food situation: we are running out of food. It will take us to 65; we can stretch it to 70, and dire at 75. Resupply to be avoided at all cost."

*A three-man rowing rotation meant two hours and fifteen minutes
at the oars, then a ninety-minute rest.* (Erinn J. Hale)

Chapter 17

—⁓—

Body and Boat Breakdown

*Lord, help me, for your sea is so big
and my boat is so small.*

—St. Brendan the Navigator

Brad listened to David Burch on the satellite phone, scribbling notes into the logbook. David's absentminded professor tone had taken on a competitive edge. He was obviously concerned but still optimistic. A week of hard work and favorable weather could boost our average speed over 2.6 knots, putting us at Falmouth under our fifty-five-day goal. A mere tenth of a knot slower would put us in a day later. David seemed confident our slowest possible average would be two knots and that at the very least we would arrive on Day 62, August 10. We continued to ration as much as we could handle.

Day 40

In the afternoon we crossed within a thousand miles of the line of longitude at Bishop Rock in the Isles of Scilly, the official end of our race. That meant a reward meal, which put everyone in a good mood. We had rowed 2179 miles, as the crow flies, from New York to England. Our actual course was considerably less direct, with storms and late-night detours made by sleepy rowers. Two days later Dylan told Emily to buy her ticket for August 4, fifteen days away. He suspected we'd arrive a day or two later. Greg talked to his girlfriend, Betsy, estimating our arrival on August 10. Rebecca had told me she would arrive on August 3. I was still the only one with a girlfriend who had not used the sat phone to communicate. We continued to write almost every day, exchanging the minutia of our alternate realities.

The next day, July 20, was Jim Wood's birthday, and I called him on the satellite phone to wish him a happy one. A week earlier I had been inspired to write my grandparents. I wrote about the second time I climbed Knocknarea with them, the summer I had turned eleven—eight years after my father's death. This would be the last time my grandmother would climb it. It had always been hard for me to tell my grandparents that I loved both of my fathers equally. I hoped this truth would not hurt them.

Their reply was typical, both sweet and laconic. My Uncle Eric, my father's younger brother and computer guru to my grandparents, had helped them read the email. It was Eric who responded with an uncharacteristically frank letter.

You are a great nephew. You show such courageous spirit. Your dad would be very proud of you. I saw your recent email to Grandpa Stan. Jordan, I am totally okay with your feelings of being the son of both Jim Hanssen and Jim Wood. Jim Wood is a great person and has been a great father for you.

We will always be very sad when thinking of the loss of your dad. There was probably a feeling that you could forget about your first dad, but that is clearly not the case. His spirit lives on with you. And you are very attached to part of Jimmy's life that he was very fond of—Sligo. I have so many great memories with your father in Sligo. I get such a great feeling when I am on top of Knocknarea thinking about all of those times.

My first memories of a man besides my father were of Uncle Eric. He was like a big, friendly giant. He took me to do all the reckless things boys enjoy, like four-wheeling, shooting guns, and blowing things up—things my mother tries not to dwell upon to this day. I was too young to consider that each time we did something fun, he probably thought a lot about my dad. I hadn't really considered my enormous uncle as someone's little brother.

Day 43

Strong winds came early on the morning of July 22. Unable to make any progress, we dropped the sea anchor. Light rain continued off and on throughout the day as each pair of rowers traded off being on deck and inside the cabin. Bundled up in our foul weather gear, we drank more coffee, occasionally getting hit by waves, and watching the clouds for airplanes and patches of blue sky.

The sunless day was turning into night, and the distant overcast horizon melted into the gray sea. This was the worst weather since Alberto. Burch wrote that "an unbelievable hodge-podge of systems" was rolling over us, with lows, highs, and fronts all converging. This shroud of uncertainty from our seemingly clairvoyant navigational coach made nightfall sinister. Hours drifted, and despite the sea anchor we floated farther and farther from the finish line. We talked, joked, sang, did crossword puzzles, and eventually drifted off into the dozens of fitful naps that characterized sea anchor sleep. Eighteen hours later, after a period longer than Tropical Storm Alberto, the weather broke enough to warrant a try behind the oars. After thirty minutes and no progress, Greg and I dropped the sea anchor in defeat. We ate breakfast self-consciously, not comfortable eating while drifting backward.

The next thirty-six hours on sea anchor would profoundly alter the success of the trip. Save for minor chores, our bedraggled bodies had been stacked like logs in the cabin or lying uncomfortably on deck. It was also the end of "rice week" before a return to polenta and mashed potatoes. We were unwisely limiting our water intake, because pissing in a bottle in a cabin with three other grown men was difficult. This was not good for anyone, but it was an especially bad recipe for Greg.

At three that afternoon the weather finally shifted, and Greg and I anxiously got on the oars. In ten minutes he was wracked in pain. He was constipated again. This time was worse than his earlier debilitating episode. The three-man shifts began immediately. Emails of cures began to flood from Seattle to the middle of the

Atlantic. We reached out to our regular onshore physician, who was not available. The doc on call did not understand the limitations of the boat. He suggested Greg eat more fruits and vegetables and walk around some more.

Other suggestions were more applicable. Greg had to get hydrated. He requisitioned one of our six-liter water bags, labeling it in permanent marker "Greg's H_2O pack of unstopability: the constipator exterminator." We never let it leave his side. His diet had to change as much as we could manage. We thought cheese was the obvious culprit, but according to the doctor, the constipation was caused by the polenta, instant mashed potatoes, and canned tuna—all our staples—on top of the rice. All foods being scarce, Greg's diet changed at the expense of Brad's, Dylan's, and my breakfast oatmeal ration (our only remaining fiber source). We each exchanged this for Greg's share of bowel-halting polenta and mashed potatoes. If things didn't change for Greg soon, much more drastic measures were in order: half a Valium, warm soapy water, a syringe, rubber glove, and a trash bag. In the back cabin, Greg followed the doctor's orders, out of view, while the rest of us continued a fear-induced coffee-drinking regimen. Our doctors reassured us that Greg was capable of holding "twenty to forty pounds of material," and that it took "weeks to die of constipation." Being weeks away from our destination, this assurance was cold comfort.

We continued to make between two and three knots. Brad, Dylan, and I did not mind hauling around a sick teammate, knowing that he would do the same for us. We restricted the use of the one iPod player to the one-man shift to keep each team communicating. Greg spent a lot of time on email, reading Burch's updates and dwelling on his inability to help. The *Yorkshire Warrior* was slowly and consistently eating into the 150-mile lead we had rebuilt since leaving the Gulf Stream. He brought up the subject while Dylan and I were on the oars.

"Do you really think that matters right now?" said Dylan incredulously, and began cranking angrily on the oars.

I looked at Greg. "I can row faster hungry than they can trying to catch us."

Day 46

Night gave way to an electric pink sunrise over purple shimmering swells. The sky and clouds reflected the same incandescent bright orange. I rowed by myself, forgetting to call Brad for his shift. I stopped to eat a meager snack. Without oars it was quiet. Half the old sailors' adage ran through my mind: "Pink skies in morning, sailors take warning." Brad crawled lethargically out of the cabin and gazed at the sunrise. We began rowing. The clouds in the distance looked like the mountain peaks on an ethereal landmass. Our strokes were short. No longer could we muscle the oar, but we continued to move.

Brad longed for the day he would not have to schedule tooth brushing hours in advance to ensure it got done. Nothing got cleaned until it demanded attention through pain or sheer disgust. And bodies were not the only things breaking down. Despite the most meticulous care, our ungrateful satellite phone—the only communication device to link us to shore—was working only half the time. Our steering system, built with a single easy-to-replace breaking point to preserve the rest of the contraption, seemed to fall apart more frequently. It felt as if the whole boat limped.

I was slowly coming to terms with the idea that our very best might not be enough. David estimated we would be onshore no later than August 10. After our last food inventory, we felt we had enough to last five days beyond that. But the ocean could keep us out here for as long as it liked. We were still more than eight hundred miles from shore.

Up until the halfway point, rationing food had seemed like a terrible discomfort and a necessary precaution. After a total of forty-two hours lost on sea anchor, as well as losing Greg for what was adding up to seventy-two hours, the possibility that we might indeed not make it to England unassisted was forcing Brad to reexamine his "biggest failure in life," as he called it. He broke it down into two categories: errors in judgment and errors in calculation. Amassing food for four full-grown men at maximum output with limited space was a huge undertaking; a miscalculation was understandable. Errors in judgment were harder for us to forgive. Like most of his projects, he had waited until the last minute and not asked for help. On the other hand, we were in this boat together; we were all guilty of a degree of negligence. Communication had broken down. We had trusted that he knew the numbers. Now he had to trust that, come what may, the rest of us could rein in our anger.

———

Later that day an email arrived from the doctor, the fifth email in the last three days addressing Greg's condition. Each subsequent message had become increasingly drastic. This last one stepped it up a notch. "Let Jordan help you out: Take a full Valium, wait an hour, then let him glove up and go to work." I'm not sure why I was singled out for the honor, but there were not enough Valiums for either of us to make this an acceptable option. Hours later, with a relief surmounting only my own, Greg shoved his way awkwardly out of the cabin to the bucket waiting for him on the port side of the boat. Everyone held their collective breath and averted their gaze. It was, according to all who observed the offending matter, the size of a fourth grader.

For five days we had either been on sea anchor or rowing with one man down. There would be no fifty-five-day record on this trip. The food crisis would continue to grow as our stores were depleted. Despite the decent miles made since lifting the sea anchor, rowing shorthanded had taken a lot out of me, Brad, and Dylan. Greg had succeeded in his task, but after a full-night's sleep he still looked worse than any of us. Gaunt and sunken-cheeked, he climbed back on the oars the next morning and started rowing.

—⁓—

Chapter 18

The Madness
of Captain Hanssen

Day 47

The specter of hunger was haunting the *James Robert Hanssen*.
We could now see the end of our stores, and what was left we
had to ration according to Burch's and our best estimate of days
remaining. Cheese, with its curse of weight and blessing of calories,
seemed like it would be with us to the bitter end. Sugar was at
a premium—the eight known candy bars remained off limits.
Powdered milk, at one point so plentiful and highly prized for its
slightly sweet flavor, had been sipped to extinction despite recent
attempts to corral consumption. All meals were made soupy to
increase the volume. What few snacks remained were reduced to a
two-ingredient combination of cheese and warm beef bouillon or
cheese and tuna.

Through this dark lens, good, even great, things seemed to be
happening. Greg was back on the oars, seemingly cured of his
affliction and regaining strength on an hourly basis. Dylan's crotch
had suffered a huge flare-up in the humid cabin during the hours
on sea anchor. For days his legs were splayed out as each stroke felt
like sandpaper. Now this too appeared to be coming under control.
The angry-looking rash had receded, although it still threatened to
erupt if he were to miss a thrice-daily washing and application of
medicine—which was also becoming scarce.

Burch estimated excellent weather and fair rowing conditions
until August 1. He noted with enthusiasm that we were over the top

Brad and I clean the bottom of the boat.

of the Mid-Atlantic Ridge, crossing from the North American plate to the Eurasian plate. This massive bathometric feature, obscured by miles of water, had no effect at the surface, yet it was impossible for us, especially for geology major Dylan, not to imagine its scope. This is the roughly eleven-thousand-mile section in the mid-Atlantic that is part of a forty-thousand-mile-long continuous mountain range, stretching into every ocean and surrounding the world like baseball stitches. In comparison, the longest continental mountain range, the Andes, is just over a tenth that length. Had this journey been made on foot, our efforts would have reached a critical juncture as we reached the top of this massive mountain range separating Europe and North America.

Intellectually, I understood that at the rate we rationed, there would be enough to row the eight hundred miles to England. Emotionally, I could not stop talking about food, describing in detail sumptuous meals of my past, from a serendipitous feast with monks at an Italian monastery with just-picked vegetables to hearty green chile stew from my mom's kitchen to the impossibly delicious, spicy butter chicken at Taste of India in Seattle. My ranting and raving had now devolved into spouting vulgar lists of food items. Our lamentations about hunger were mentioned copiously in video diaries and the logbook—every place we could register complaints that would not make their way back to our families. The lunatic food ravings of their mad captain were crushing the crew, and I remained blind to the silence that met my vocal imagination.

Brad saw my suffering as self-imposed, but I was inflicting it on him too. So he blocked me out. Dealing with his guilt had hardened him. We were not eating enough to sustain our weight. At the crew's average height of six foot three and fighting weight of two hundred pounds each, we needed a little over twenty-five hundred calories to maintain that weight in an inactive life style. These numbers are based on the Harris-Benedict Equation developed in 1918. While all simple equations have their limitations, this formula remains a reasonably accurate estimation. Working out twice a day, six to seven days a week while we trained for college rowing increased this number to four thousand calories. Twelve hours rowing every day with little sleep took it to an entirely different level.

We chose to know hunger. At any time we could have let Woodvale and our families know what we were enduring, and the pain would be fixed within days. But we would not tolerate an assisted row. I had come to the decision to forgive Brad, but each time I looked at him, I just couldn't. Declaring my anger toward him a few weeks earlier had seemed necessary, but it was ultimately unsatisfying. As much as my rage, disappointment, and desire pumped vitriol through my heart, I did not want to wait until we were safe on shore to forgive him. If we made it, then what weight would forgiveness carry? If we didn't make it, I didn't know if I was strong enough to say it and mean it.

It would be a few more days before I switched rowing partners back to Brad. If I could forgive him, I wanted it to be private, and there was no way to take him aside until we rowed together. I did not know if forgiving him would mean that I could trust him again. But if I didn't trust him, was it actually forgiveness?

Day 49

Spray blasted us as the tumultuous quick seas pushed us under low clouds. We struggled with short, quick strokes. Every half dozen strokes the oars were knocked from the riggers. Handles were shoved into our stomachs and beat our shins. Nothing precluded normal conversation or our metronome cadence save the resetting of the oar. Clouds marched before the wind, revealing bright blue sky that warmed our backs, and the waters changed from gray to cobalt. When a large enough wave revealed itself, we paused the oars to let the swell take the hull with a whoosh of bubbling water.

It was July 28, and today the edge of Europe made its way onto the tiny GPS receiver screen. In celebration, we added the Hasselhoff dinners to the menu. Each one of these was about 250 to 330 extra calories. All had different flavors and some were sweet. Six hundred forty miles left to go; as the five-hundred-mile mark approached, we felt more comfortable about our rations. We had asked David Burch to find out what our slowest five hundred miles had been (thirteen days), so fifteen days seemed a reasonable estimate for the last five hundred. The extra rations boosted everyone's spirits. Dylan was amazed at the joy a few hundred calories could add to his experience.

Day 50

The morning arrived with the same hard but blessedly quick rowing. August 10 was twelve days away, and we figured we could easily cover five hundred miles at a paltry 1.75-knot average. Even better, we had rationed enough food to accommodate five days beyond that. Nature proved generous. Earlier that morning a small fish had the misfortune to wash up on deck. Our best guess was that it was a baby swordfish. No one appeared interested, but to me it looked like it had enough meat for four or five bites. I offered my crewmates a share of the bounty, but Dylan and Greg were more than happy to leave me this culinary pleasure. Brad looked at me skeptically as I prepared to clean the fish.

You might be wondering why we were not fishing full time for more calories. The primary reason was that we were participating in a race. Persistence was the best strategy to win: not just harder rowing but more physical time behind the oars. Pulling up a fish on the tiny deck of the boat seemed like a very messy, time-consuming, and potentially dangerous experience. Because of that, fishing equipment was classified as auxiliary equipment. As we grew hungrier, however, the thought of pulling up a fish and devouring it on the spot sounded incredibly appealing...but impossible. We had taken the boat apart three times to look for the package of hand reels, hooks, and line, to no avail. Eventually we came to a conclusion about the one event that could have caused its loss.

"If it's not on the boat, we don't need it," Dylan had said on the dock in New Jersey after my brother Douglas had fallen in, taking with him a white trash bag with contents unknown. Only now did we suspect that this unknown bag held the fishing equipment.

Now this little blue and silver fish had made its way onto the deck without the trouble of a hook and line. Gutting it proved no problem. I chopped it through the spine into five fine-looking bites of fish that I cooked in boiling water before adding polenta and butter. It tasted like sole mixed with swordfish: excellent.

Life was good. England seemed just over the horizon. Food would hold and I had eaten fresh fish. I brewed myself a large cup of coffee, quite happy to sit on deck in the sun and enjoy a post-breakfast caffeine kick. Medium-sized waves crashed over the gunwales every five minutes for what seemed like hours on end. Brad and Dylan looked haggard. I sipped my coffee in silence, content to exist on deck, gazing into the partly cloudy, endless horizon. I made a point not to listen to their conversation, which was about food. As far as I was concerned, we had rerationed and the few hundred extra calories I would get per day was good enough to get me to England.

"Now we're counting grits as a breakfast?" Dylan's sharp tone grabbed my attention.

"Yes, grits for breakfast," replied Brad.

"There's no instant breakfast or fruit snacks in those packs?"

"No, there's not," said Brad patiently. Sugar was the real issue.

Dylan was visibly agitated and pulled a few more strokes before he replied. "Brad, you really fucked up."

The adrenaline-fueled boat speed picked up and silence settled. What had pushed Dylan over the edge amounted to a lack of an extra 210 calories at breakfast time. We had chosen to count the grits as a breakfast pack, but unlike with the granola and oatmeal breakfast packets, days we had grits would mean no sugar. Dylan had not caught this detail during our last rerationing. The realization that sugar would have to wait another twenty-four hours brought his anger to a head.

As uncomfortable as this exchange was to watch, something about it was supremely satisfying. I grinned, trying to hide the inappropriate reaction by bringing the coffee to my lips, thankful for my wide dark sunglasses. Dylan's public railing not only made Brad uncomfortable, but it also revealed a kinship of human frailty that had been hidden from me until now. For weeks Dylan's unflappable nature had impressed me to the point that I felt terrible about my own rage. I thought my inability to let go of anger was unique to me. Observing Dylan's fury was oddly reassuring.

It also showed me what my outburst at Brad would have looked like to a third party, and I could see both perspectives more clearly. Brad could only apologize so much. I could not in good conscience use his one major mistake to fault him every time he irritated me. Like everyone else, Brad was doing everything in his capacity to get us to England. As much as we might want to berate him the entire way, it wasn't productive, nor was it right.

Minutes after his outburst, Dylan apologized. He would not bring it up anymore. Brad viewed each outburst lobbed at him as a test. He knew his position on the boat was not one from which to issue orders or to complain. The question was how he could be an asset. He concluded he would absorb the anger. If we were mad at him, we could be less angry at each other.

Day 53

We rowed within the five-hundred-mile barrier on August 1. Our fastest five hundred miles had been out of New York, in a blistering eight days. Both David Burch and Woodvale, who rarely agreed, estimated that we would arrive nine days from now. Dylan and Brad had recently spied a seagull. This was a good omen. These birds lived on the coast and this gull could only have come from Europe. It was our first natural confirmation of land.

We had 481 miles to go. It was cool enough for jackets but not yet cold. Greg and Brad rowed through the motions, distracted by our conversation. Dylan sat on deck, pencil in hand, going over numbers in our little yellow book. I documented the happy occasion from the cabin. Dylan made his last few notes on the waterproof paper. We were silent as we weighed the consequences.

"We started rationing on Day 18," said Greg. Once more the food had been meticulously counted and rerationed for our latest arrival estimation. Records no longer mattered, eclipsed by the joy of eating almost enough for the first time in thirty-five days. Breakfast had been counted out for eleven days. In our possession were seven oatmeal packets each, with their instant breakfast shake and fruit snacks, and four packets of sugarless grits. On two of the grits days, each rower would get three fig bars. For the next ten days each man would get one additional ration of Hasselhoff breakfast. Four instant mashed potato dinners with four six-ounce tuna packs would be saved for emergency breakfasts if we were still out here past August 11. Dinner was even better: we had thirteen polentas and four fancy dehydrated meals to celebrate each hundred-mile milestone, plus an extra Hasselhoff dinner for the next ten days. This amounted to a little over fifteen days of full breakfasts and dinners.

But for just the next ten days, we had even more. For extra snacks we had a bag of savory cereal mix, a bag of pretzels, a full snack pack good for two days, and two MREs (meals ready to eat) per rower. These military combat rations can be eaten hot or cold. They are the result of almost sixty years of the military trying to create a complete meal with enough calories and nutrition that can be stored for years—and that soldiers will actually eat. It's asking a lot out of food. Each MRE contained roughly twelve hundred calories and was expected to count for an entire day's snacks for lunch and late night. These would be consumed any two days of our choice. There was enough cheese for each rower to have eight hundred calories, for eighteen days—although a considerable amount would be lost to mold. Every hundred miles, or an estimated two days, we would get three cream cheese packets at an extra hundred calories each. At 250 miles to go, each rower would get twelve cheese sticks for an extra eighty calories each.

Even if the last five hundred miles lasted two days longer than our previous longest five hundred miles (thirteen days), we would suck up the lack of variety. Better to be nourished now to speed to England. We considered these "full meals," and they added roughly twelve hundred to eighteen hundred calories per day. Our consumption jumped up to between thirty-two hundred and thirty-eight hundred calories for ten days—enough to eat a little bit after each rowing shift.

The torture had ended. "Guys, we got through it!" I nearly wept. The turning point had to be acknowledged. Everyone agreed the estimations were conservative, and three days from now was my twenty-fourth birthday—things could not get any better. We were 250 miles up on our competition, and we had continued to gain miles throughout our starvation, constipation, and time on the sea anchor. For the first time since Day 17, we rowed the ocean without distraction.

—〰—

Chapter 19

Bottleneck

Day 54

Genteel swells clothed in silky blue water obscured the horizon of the monochrome dawn. Eighty feet above the surface of the ocean, on the bridge of the radish-colored 540-foot freighter *Hood Island*, the details on the surface of the water were less distinct. This was the second ship we had seen in as many days from the Port of Antwerp bound for the eastern seaboard, with hundreds of containers of general cargo. The freighter's journey had begun about a thousand miles away. In less than twenty-four hours it passed Falmouth, and in the following twenty-four it had steamed another four hundred miles toward us. Although the *Hood Island*'s speed was lightning quick compared with ours, the journey was anything but exceptional. The Port of Antwerp, nestled fifty miles inland, can handle ships twice as long and several times the volume of the *Hood Island*. This freighter could hold 218 of our little vessels. Its presence was indicative of an increasing danger of ship collision.

The crew of the *Hood Island* did not see us as it emerged from the fog a mile behind our vessel. The officer on deck politely let us know he changed course because of the small unidentifiable blip that showed up on his radar. The freighter passed within a quarter mile of our stern. Fifty-four other ports along the English Channel and the North Sea dump hundreds of ships into this shipping channel every day. We were headed toward a hundred-mile-wide

Brad checks weather on the computer in the stern cabin.

choke point of worldwide commerce, with hundreds of ships that nevertheless have little to fear from each other, since for several years commercial vessels over three hundred tons have been required to use the Automatic Identification System (AIS). This technology uses radio signals to send out a consistent signal with the ship's name, position, and heading, and is updated constantly on other ships' communications equipment. But the *James Robert Hanssen* could not create the power to support this system—we relied primarily on sight and our active radar responder.

Dozens of airplanes soared overhead, and now the multiple daily ship sightings inspired dreams of shore. Falmouth is situated roughly twenty-five miles east of the westernmost edge of England on the Cornish peninsula. It sits on the shore of the world's third largest natural harbor, the first large safe place to land in mainland England from the North Atlantic.

Until Henry the VIII's divorce habit emphasized the defensive value of the area, it was little more than a small fishing settlement on Carrak Roads, the largest tidal estuary in Britain. Henry's excommunication from the Church in Rome gave all "good" Catholic empires like France and Spain carte blanche to invade England, with the goal of reinstating the Catholic Church as England's one true religion. By the time he made it to his fifth wife, Henry was in the midst of a building program of thirty coastal castles for defense, including Pendennis and St. Mawes on either side of the entrance to Falmouth harbor.

It remained a strategic backwater until 1688 and the age of sail. The fast and lightly armed packet ships brought the news of the world and the British Empire's expanding dominion to Falmouth. Its convenient location was easier and safer to consistently sail into rather than beating up the English Channel into London. Upon arrival, the news was thrown into a coach and hurried off the two hundred miles to London to arrive a week later. Falmouth would know the latest before the king, the queen, and Parliament. For a century and a half, this relatively obscure town hosted the likes of Benjamin Franklin, Napoleon, and Charles Darwin, and developed a taste for the worldly, adventurous, and cosmopolitan—and most important, fast sailing ships. By the mid-1800s steamships, which were less beholden to the winds, had developed enough to fight their way up the English Channel in any weather with enough consistency to steam straight to London. Thus the golden age of the Falmouth packet ships came to an end.

—⁓—

Dylan's mother Linda had arrived in Falmouth on July 26. She was staying in town, regularly sending Dylan vivid descriptions of the local scene. Greg's parents, Dave and Marie, showed up four days later. They had rented a house just outside of town with my parents and brother, who were joining them that afternoon. Keven and Meg Vickers, Brad's parents, would be joining his uncle, Peter, at his cottage just outside of Falmouth. In the next twenty-four hours, Dylan's father Ron and his girlfriend Charlene would also join the growing OAR Northwest fan club.

All of the girlfriends—Betsy, Emily, and Rebecca—had landed in the United Kingdom by this time. Instead of waiting around for us to complete the row, they had decided to explore the UK before settling in Falmouth. Betsy took the train up to Scotland to run a half marathon and visit some friends, while Rebecca and Emily explored London.

The documentary film crew had been in England for a few weeks. Todd and Kathy had spent the summer glued to the computer between filming interviews of our parents and heading to Ballard to film navigator Burch in his weather lair. Since arriving, they had been shooting B-roll film and doing interviews between London and Cornwall. Erinn, our still photographer, was couch-surfing in London until we got closer. The only one not yet on English soil was Brad's childhood friend Chris Cohen. Chris had seen us off in New York and would touch down in a few days.

The emotional gravity of our lives had shifted to a tiny town in Cornwall we had never seen. I was concerned that I would not get to see my dad and my brother, though they had immediately extended their stay through August 15 upon landing. As of our latest estimate, we hoped to cross the fifty-mile-long finish gate at Bishop

Rock Lighthouse on August 9. Attached to the end of a thirty-two-hundred-mile race, an extra seventy miles remained to Falmouth to achieve the first unassisted mainland United States to mainland UK crossing, which seemed like it would take perhaps a day and a half at most. With limited food, breaking that record loomed larger than it had fifty-four days ago.

Time with my brother and father would be limited. Rebecca was staying only through August 18. My mother, however, assured me that she would stay as long as was needed to see me safe on shore. This was a great comfort, but the thought of not having all of my family to share the end as I had imagined it meant I had something more to lose.

Days 54 and 55

Greg's thin face had filled in with a considerable auburn bristle, and his hair had morphed into a mop of white blond unseen since his childhood. He contemplated our position—now 350 miles from the gate at Bishop Rock Lighthouse—and thought of the two Norwegians from New Jersey who had propelled themselves to that point 110 years earlier. Almost a month ago we had crossed the halfway point. To get there, it had taken us under thirty days, during which we had spent nearly forty-eight total hours on sea anchor absorbing hurricane-force winds, avoiding lightning, and searching for the Gulf Stream. At the time, crossing in fifty-five days seemed reasonable, but the last three weeks of unfavorable weather and sickness had put that record beyond our reach. If the weather held, at least we would match the Dutch crew, although that would feel like second place.

We felt foolish comparing ourselves to Harbo and Samuelsen. Our adventure paled next to the risk they had undertaken: we had double the crew, a water maker, an EPIRB, and an inflatable life raft. People thought we were crazy, but few imagined we would perish. Fellow boatmen on the Hudson who bid adieu to Harbo and Samuelsen in New York were certain, according to a contemporary *New York Times* article, that "their destination was *Davy Jones Locker.*" Yet to attribute their feat as superhuman would take away their humanity and the lifetime of work on the sea that each had put in to accomplish this feat.

Since Chay Blyth and John Ridgeway rowed the Atlantic in 1966, eleven more men and one woman had crossed the North Atlantic before us—all inspired and united by the odd desire to row an ocean. If you add the much shorter crossings from Newfoundland, it's twenty-two men and two women who have crossed the North Atlantic. Since Harbo and Samuelsen, no one had embarked on this journey to see if it was humanly possible; we needed to know if we were personally capable of such a feat.

Adventuring for its own sake rather than to explore, exploit, fight, or convert is a relatively modern phenomenon, and in some ways this made it a selfish endeavor. It certainly affected our desire to pair the trip with a charity. Yet I was surprised to see that even without the charity most folks had enthusiastically agreed we should do it, and that now was the time. They donated money and services so that they too would have a stake in our success. It was the most basic of stories—young men on a quest—almost trite in the metaphoric details. Each donation was a statement of goodwill combined with a tinge of envy at our privilege of completing a task purely for the virtue of the challenge.

Regardless of the philosophical worth of our trip, a small decision made by Harbo and Samuelsen left the door open just wide enough for a different team to claim a different world record. Their stop in the Isles of Scilly before making it to the French port of Le Havre five days later meant we would be the first to row from mainland USA to mainland UK. It was not the record we had originally hoped for, but it still allowed our project the cachet of "record-breaking row" as well as the marketing phrase "first Americans."

The obsession with breaking the record came out of our commitment to the hundreds of people and dozens of companies who had invested in our success. We were driven to bring back some distinction on top of rowing the ocean. Certainly egotistical desire drove us, but so did an optimistic naïveté that our labors behind the oars might have a lasting impact beyond ourselves.

—∿∿—

The newest, unexpected addition to our fan club in the UK was Greg's sister Angie, who was to fly to England on August 7. Greg lit up at this news. Like many siblings, they had grown closer as adults and wished they saw more of each other. Perhaps it was the remoteness of the ocean, but Greg reflected on how little he had seen Angie in the past two years. She had been lukewarm to the idea of him rowing the ocean. Greg had a much easier time persuading his parents that this was more than a passing fancy. Up until the day we departed New York, she was not convinced. With fewer than five hundred miles to go, Angie's decision to make this trip meant more to Greg than any words of approval she could have sent.

PART FIVE

My birthday in the middle of the Atlantic

—∿∿—

Chapter 20

Birthday Treats

Day 56

It was the afternoon of August 4—my twenty-fourth birthday. For my special day I was allowed first dibs from the eight random MREs. I chose vegetable manicotti, not for the manicotti but for the "wheat snack bread." It was the only piece of bread on the boat and would become the body of my birthday cake. Laid out before me in the cabin were two packets of cream cheese, one packet of real sugar from the MRE, some fruit snacks left over from breakfast, a fig bar, manicotti, and some matches, also from the MRE. I decided to eat the manicotti first. MREs can be eaten cold, but this was a birthday meal, so I took the extra time to heat up the Mylar bag in boiling water.

In the midst of heating the manicotti in the camp stove, I felt the urge to relieve myself. Instead of turning off the burner and taking two steps to do this outside, I asked Greg for the pee bottle. Without a word, he handed it to me and I multitasked with practiced efficiency. I sealed the lid and handed the bottle to Greg—completing the entire operation with one hand. He emptied the bottle and called back into the cabin. "Can you pass me a cream cheese packet, please?" This unquestionably unsanitary behavior no longer registered as unacceptable.

My manicotti was lukewarm when I opened it. The Mylar had done its job and reflected the heat, but in the wrong direction. Still, I devoured its mushy contents. I squeezed the last of the tomato sauce into my mouth and eyed the remaining ingredients before me. I opened two packets of cream cheese and cautiously tasted them. Both seemed safe from the rancidness that tainted about 10 percent of our supply. Satisfied, I squeezed the contents into the plastic bag along with the precious sugar packet. I stirred the mixture with my finger, creating a frosting. With the gusto of a celebrity chef, I placed the little red and orange fruit snacks into the frosting—it was fantastic. I even had tiny birthday candles—matches left over from the MRE. Greg insisted I display my creation.

"You should *definitely* take a picture of that," said Brad. I handed him the camera and began singing myself "Happy Birthday" for the second time in fifteen minutes.

Greg turned to Brad and mouthed the word "psycho" before turning back to me for a picture.

—⁓—

Later I opened a birthday card Rebecca had given me back in Seattle. She had written it two months earlier with the hope that by this time we might be in Falmouth celebrating my birthday together. I had still not talked to Rebecca. The phone conversations between Greg and Dylan and their girlfriends seemed to me a frustratingly poor facsimile of intimacy. Even with my parents, I found the phone much less satisfying than writing. Taking the time to reflect on each thought was far more meaningful and comforting to me. It was also private, unlike the overheard phone calls. By now, however, I realized this was not good enough for Rebecca. Communication via the sat phone was becoming more unreliable as the saltwater environment continued to corrode the electrical connections. Now I judged using it an unnecessary use of mission-critical equipment. I hoped Rebecca would understand.

—⁓—

According to David Burch, the weather was looking pretty good, with an equally good chance of a lot of unfavorable wind. Fortunately his advice was a bit more concrete than the weather forecast. Given the many ship sightings, he reminded us "to keep full concentration on all details until the boat is tied to the dock." He recounted several disasters that had occurred on the last or next to last day of an ocean crossing. "There is a very common tendency," he explained, "in a difficult ocean passage to start to relax once the perceived hard part is over."

That afternoon Burch wrote us that he had examined our past progress and discovered that it would take only a very light northerly wind to keep us from heading northeast. We knew this, but David outlined the implications. England and the foot of the fifty-mile finish gate, starting at Bishop Rock and heading south, was still northeast. If a north wind began to blow, we would not cross the gate but pass below it, forcing us to backtrack and head back up and around to finish. This would waste an incredible amount of time, and our limited stores might make turning around impossible. North winds were due in a few days, the very edge of an accurate prediction. Right now, getting north was more important than going east. To play it safe, we would have to change our eastward course to the north by at least sixty miles.

Before midnight the stars worked their way out from behind the clouds. Greg and I rowed. Looking into the smoky hatch, I wondered why Dylan and Brad had not gone to sleep yet. Dylan opened it up, and he and Brad scrambled out. "Are we ready to do this?" he asked.

"Jordan, stop rowing," Greg said, tapping me on the shoulder. "Ship the oars, man," said Brad.

Dylan shoved a warm Jetboil stove into my hand with a flare duct-taped to it. Into the other hand he gave me a headlamp and some bits of paper and the three of them began to belt out happy birthday. They presented me with "Mum's best apple custard," the last Hasselhoff dessert. Along with the white nonemergency flare, this was my real birthday cake and candle. The homemade birthday card was built from extra sheets in our waterproof logbook and a binding made of duct tape, and strong polymer twine. On the front was a hand-drawn picture of our rowboat with three stick figures riding atop two large blue waves. One of them, wearing my wide-brimmed leather hat and long hair, had a speech bubble: "Ladies and Gentlemen, today I am closer to..." I flipped the card over to see a close-up of a larger stick figure with even longer locks and another speech bubble: "...being a bad ass mother because I just turned twenty-four in the middle of the ocean—on a rowboat!"

Dylan had found a blue pen somewhere on the boat and had taken a lot of his time, without me knowing—a miracle in itself on this small craft—smudging the ink to fill in the waves. This detail blew me away. They'd all signed the card, keeping it and the last extra custard out of sight for several days. Planning the surprise in secrecy was a feat of coordination between the three of them. For the first time since Day 17, Brad, told me later, he felt like part of the team.

Day 57

In the early gray dawn I filmed Greg and Dylan chucking hunks of cheese into a sedate North Atlantic. I could not argue that the fuzzy blocks did not look disgusting. At my suggestion that they were salvageable, they cackled and let two more blocks fly. Hard cheese is one of the few items the USDA says you can save by cutting at least one inch back from the mold. This is, of course, a greater mental leap when said cheese is completely covered. Really, it all depends on hunger level and desperation. Their wrath toward the hairy dairy products had not changed. Tossing it seemed to be a loosely justified cathartic necessity.

My constant food chatter had weakened my credibility, and I balanced just how important a battle this was to fight. If I asserted my authority, I knew Dylan and Greg would resist. I would have had Brad on my side, but his opinion on food did not carry a whole lot of weight. We were now scheduled to come in on August 11, six days from now. I watched silently as two days' ration of cheese— sixty-four-hundred calories—perhaps half of that salvageable, in my opinion, descended toward the abyss of the Celtic Sea.

Later that morning, the freighter *Nord de la Monde* passed within a mile of us. Greg caught the captain in a congenial mood and explained our mission. The captain's response on the VHF could be heard on deck. "My God! Fifty-seven days! My God!" He repeated this several times, to our great amusement. At our current intake, we had eight days of food left.

—⁓—

Two subjects dominated Dylan's mind: how much he loved and felt energized by eating two breakfasts a day, and his aching, purple crotch rot. As long as he could eat two breakfasts and wash twice a day, he could make it to England.

Under an overcast sky around noontime, another email came from David. In capital letters he emphasized his opinion: "COULD BE A VERY LATE FINISH IF YOU DO NOT GET ABOVE THE FINISH GATE IN NEXT COUPLE DAYS." We had held out on his earlier advice, hoping to get another more favorable weather report and maintain a satisfying eastern progress. With this new warning, we made it our business to get north. Burch's emails cast another blanket of uncertainty around us. I thought of my full stomach over the past few days and wondered if I should feel guilty. A lot could happen in three hundred miles on the North Atlantic.

—∿∿—

As the thought of missing my dad in Falmouth became real, I resolved that I needed to spend more time with him after all this was over. Not in England but in life. I would get to England when I got there, and he would stay as long as he could. That, I could not control. I could not help not knowing Jim Hanssen, but I could make more time for Jim Wood.

Dusk settled into evening. I felt like another food discussion might crush me, but David's report on the weather's unending fickleness had potentially shattered our rerationing estimate of five days earlier. It was still warm enough for Brad to sit on deck shirtless, with our yellow logbook to lead the discussion. "How many days do we want to count to, because right now we're good until the fifteenth," he asked. "Do we want to add five days?"

This idea sounded prudent. Our rations had been an acceptable thirty-two to thirty-eight hundred calories a day—a little bit less than what the U.S. military suggests for a day of strenuous work. Since then we'd had a huge boost in both morale and energy. Tonight we would come within three hundred miles of the finish line, with seventy miles to Falmouth after that. We had to decide how our ten days of mostly full rations could be stretched another five.

Through some Hanukkah-like miracle we discovered three extra oatmeal dinners and one extra packet of grits hiding on the boat.

That meant we had fourteen full breakfasts that could take us to August 19. Combined with found food and adding the three hundred-mile meals, our dinner count jumped to sixteen days (to August 21). Since the beginning of the month, we had plowed through half of our eighty Hasselhoffs at two a day. We halved the ration so they would last another five days.

Most troubling was the cheese. There were ten days left at the usual eight ounces per rower. We would eat half rations, or four ounces instead of eight ounces—a drop of four hundred calories. This put us around twenty-four hundred calories for at least the next three days. If the weather changed and we could add more cheese, it would take us up to around twenty-eight hundred calories. Not as bad as a week ago, when we were at two thousand calories a day, but my stomach ached at the thought of another reduction.

Clean-shaven and wearing new team uniforms, we launched for the first time eight months before the race—an optimistic time that is now hard to remember.

Chapter 21

Food and Forgiveness

Day 59

Dylan stood up on deck for a better view and counted aloud the stationary lights around us. One, two, three, four, five, and six right next to him...and the seventh and eighth—over there. The moon was so bright its light filtered out all but the brightest stars, making the rest of the sky appear black and empty. Not since New York had we seen more than two ships on the horizon, and they were always moving. For five hours we rowed within sight of the lights of those ships. The VHF was silent on every possible public channel. We chose silence as well.

Greg's body seemed to be breaking down the most, even compared with Dylan's debilitating rash. He suspected he'd lost at least thirty pounds. A scraped knee had reopened and settled into an angry infection that would stay with him until he had enough food and rest on shore. His large and muscular legs had shrunk so much that the spandex shorts, normally form-fitting, were visibly loose. The new round of food rationing had yet to take a toll. Despite this, especially in light of having to row with Brad the past few days, Greg appeared upbeat. They had developed a mutual toleration to endure each other until shore. Even this was not without its difficulties. Greg was capable of filling the entire two-hour shift with chatter. And Brad could row two hours in silence and not feel uncomfortable. The result was Greg trying very hard to get Brad out of his "awkward" shell, and Brad indulging Greg's "compulsion" to talk. The whole process appeared remarkably congenial, with brief glimpses of mutual interest and enjoyment. This made their four-day rowing shifts, shackled together, slightly more bearable.

Brad noted that the boat was down to three pounds of coffee and two pounds of Gatorade powder, the two predominant items consumed between lunch and dinner. There was less fear about drinking through the coffee; running out of Gatorade would be the real tragedy. Whatever electrolytes and other science might be in it was overshadowed by its generous amount of sugar. It was good in water, but I had found pouring a scoop into my mouth like eating sweet-tart dust. This too was coming to an end.

—◠◡◠—

For more than a day we rowed north, actually slightly northwest, a completely different direction by almost 160 degrees from the shores of merry England. North winds were coming tomorrow, according to Burch, and might stay for several days. If we did not get north, we could get blown below the finish gate. Dylan and Greg made good time. It was sunny, almost cheerful, despite the dark clouds brooding on the horizon. For now it was a beautiful morning and they were talking about my favorite subject: food.

"Dylan, let me tell you about SoupSpoon," said Greg. We'd been playing a "make up a restaurant" game for days now, Greg's attempt to get me to talk about food more creatively. At Greg's SoupSpoon restaurant the portions were huge. Greg had convinced himself that he would actually open such a restaurant. Dylan had not played yet and was intrigued.

"It's an everyday place," Greg continued, "with homemade soup made daily with fresh seasonal ingredients. Our signature is a smoked salmon chowder...."

Chowder, I thought. *What goes best with chowder?* This was awesome, and I had not even come up with the game. Finally they got it! Imagining food was almost as good as eating it!

"You can eat in, or you can call up and have it ready to pick up on your way home from work." He went on, describing décor and regular patrons. "It's not a fancy place; you can wear jeans and a T-shirt, or if you wear a suit you walk in after work with your tie undone. There's a small bar. It's no place for a big crowd. Behind the bar is a big chalkboard where the menu is handwritten each day."

I nodded in approval, imagining myself walking into SoupSpoon from a rainy, cool Seattle afternoon, giving my buddy Greg a high-five and then settling down to a vat of chowder.

"This kitchen is immaculate. It's industrial but cozy, with all stainless steel pans." He went on about kitchen design and appliances, getting farther and farther away from the good stuff. Greg had gone off course. This was SoupSpoon—where was the soup? I needed to get this conversation back on track.

"I love my mom's cornbread!" I blurted. It would almost certainly go well with the chowder at SoupSpoon. Silence descended on the boat. Dylan and Greg stopped rowing.

"Jordan, you can't just randomly list food," said Greg firmly. Apparently 1200 calories was all that separated me from my grip on sanity.

Dylan agreed with Greg. "Seriously, Jordan. This is hurting us. We can't handle it; it makes it harder for everybody. You can't talk about food anymore."

This was how I handled the hunger. I needed this. I had no idea what I would do without my food talk. But I had just begun to realize how much my coping mechanism had turned into a neurosis. I mumbled a weak apology. Feeling ashamed, I nodded silently in understanding. I stood on deck awkwardly for several more minutes to make my entrance into the cabin less of a retreat.

———

The weather remained pleasant but continued to come from the wrong direction. In the day and a half since David's suggestion to go north, we had traveled sixty miles and made it to the latitude of the midpoint of the finish gate, still roughly 250 miles away. With no need to go north any more, we began heading southeast, then rowing north to gain a few miles. Tedious as the zigzagging was, it was a strategy for progress.

For hours we kept the bow of the boat toward England. Despite this, we actually advanced southeast toward France. When we turned north to gain the lost latitude, any forward motion would not let us go directly north but rather northwest. To maintain our position, we were rowing back and forth, northwest to southeast and back again. We could not afford to row any farther north or south. Sea anchor was not an option. Putting it in the water meant we would drift, and with our location now absolutely critical, no one wanted to let our fortunes follow the current. We would row this treadmill from hell and maintain our position until the wind changed or we ran out of food—whichever came first.

Brad and I had about ten minutes before the sunset shift—the best shift of the day. It was cold and we'd donned our long pants, jackets, and knit caps. Brad looked like a castaway. His cheeks above his ruddy beard were wind-beaten red. His eyes were slightly sunken in with sleep deprivation, and his bright white eyebrows stood out in contrast. We sat in the cabin for our final moments of rest. He'd just made a cup of coffee.

"Brad?" I asked quietly.

He looked up from pressing the coffee. "What's up, man? Want some coffee?"

I nodded, sipping the hot, bitter liquid. I felt like I was about to remove a millstone that had been hanging around my neck for forty-two days. He cocked his head, looking at me curiously.

"I need you to know," I said, "whatever happens out here, I forgive you for the food."

Brad's face twisted with emotion. Tears fell from my eyes. My heart and gut seemed to loosen as if the giant fist that had been clutching them suddenly let go. "I have to do this now," I explained, "because forgiveness would mean less on shore. I'm sorry it's taken so long."

It was the closest I'd ever seen Brad come to crying. He smiled and thanked me. I patted him on the shoulder in lieu of the full-on horizontal man hug that would feel a bit too romantic in the confines of the cabin. He headed out on deck. I wiped the tears from my eyes.

Brad and I had known each other for nearly six years. Without him, this idea of rowing the ocean would have gone down as a pipe dream. Whatever record we would or would not get was not worth losing his friendship. Part of not wanting to forgive him for so long was the ego of wanting to get across the ocean. Ego still drove desire, but not at that price.

Before following Brad on deck, I pulled a picture out of a small album Rebecca had given me. Most of the photos were of her and of us together. There were some random shots of the team, with little text bubbles that strung together a loose narrative documenting the eighteen months before the race. One of those pictures was of the four crewmates taken nine months earlier. There was not a whisker between us. We wore four geeky smiles and the same cheap, ill-fitting yellow rain slicks and blue knit caps. I'd purchased these so the four of us could have some semblance of a matching uniform before we put our brand-new ocean rowboat in the water. Rebecca had penned a one-word caption on the photo: "Friends." I took the photo out from its safe case in the album and stuck it under some wires on the bulkhead, where it was visible to all. I went out to row.

Greg holds up one of the gooseneck barnacles and its calcified float.

—w—

Ithaca

Day 60

"When I see this, I think I'm in someone else's world," Greg said
quietly. He and Dylan swayed with a drunklike stagger as they peered
into the water. Around us, below us, and as far as we could see into
the water were hundreds of thousands of the same strange, opaque,
cylindrical objects. Throughout our journey we would pass through
patches of flora and fauna too large to be plankton just under the
surface. They were large, easy to see with the naked eye from the
deck of the rowboat. The first of these had been sargassum, the tan-
brown seaweed we'd dubbed ocean tumbleweed. Later, floating golf
balls appeared. Upon closer inspection, they were more of a dirty
off-white color and hard to the touch. Attached in clusters of one to
five were buoy barnacles—long, slender, clam-shaped crustaceans
hanging from the bottom of the boat. When the creatures are young,
free-floating zooplankton, they eventually attach to whatever small
natural or man-made object floats by. A hard, cementlike foam will
cover the object, creating a natural life preserver from which these
tiny colonies can travel across the ocean. Our latest visitors were
even stranger.

"There's one on your oar," Greg pointed out. Without water to
hold up its boneless body, the opaque object, with an odd lumpy,
ochre substance on one side, hung limply off the blade. In the water
it filled out into a tubelike shape four to five inches long.

"It totally looks like spent condoms," said Greg. They floated alone or in groups of up to a hundred or more, side by side, in ten-foot spirals three feet across. They were suspended at random angles to each other in the water. "Or pictures of distant galaxies."

Ideas and images floated unanchored in our minds before, unfiltered, the thought made its way to speech. Our theories on what these beasts could be ranged from some kind of jellyfish to strange fish eggs, but they were neither. Despite a jellyfishlike appearance and touch, it turns out the "salp" is not even in the same phylum. It is a chordate, the same phylum as humans, thanks to the presence of a larval notochord, but of the subphylum tunicate. The notochord is a prespine similar to what other vertebrates have in their embryonic state. The salp never developed beyond this most basic state.

The salp is actually quite common. Swarms of up to billions can eat thousands of tons of phytoplankton per day via internal filters. Using one of the most efficient pumps in nature to both feed and move itself, these tiny gluttons procreate in such great numbers that the volume of their waste and dead carcasses falling to the bottom of the ocean removes a measurable portion of earth's carbon from the surface of the water, dropping it deep into the ocean and out of circulation for hundreds of years. We rowed through them for miles, knowing nothing at the time beyond the visual inspiration and presence of these alien creatures—evidence that we remained deep in another world.

⸺⁓⸺

We'd rowed 254 miles in eight days. We'd covered 179 of those miles in three days. We'd pulled and prodded a mere seventy-five miles in the four days since then—a speed of less than one knot. Traveling northbound, almost parallel to the finish line, we grabbed a mere six miles east over the past day. Between the wee hours of August 8 and midmorning, we'd already more than doubled yesterday's progress. Not great speed, but it was east, and on a sunny warm day, it was worth celebrating.

In a recent email sent from shore, skipper Mark Terry and his *Sula* crewmates assured us that it was okay we were taking our time: England was "completely overrated." The damage *Sula* had sustained in Tropical Storm Alberto had compounded concerns for the problematic vessel. For the sake of the hull and the souls on board Mark had headed into port before they got themselves into any real danger, leaving the rowers in their sturdy boats to battle the elements alone.

Meanwhile, Simon Chalk, the race organizer, was scrambling to find another craft to act as safety vessel. This meant that the sailboat that had just appeared on the horizon was unrelated to our race. We could see people on it—unlike on the large metal fortresses powering by us with disturbing regularity. The ocean we had imagined had many more small sailboats on it. Save for *Sula*'s two visits, this was not the case. A palpable excitement at the prospect of meeting new people ran through the boat. I called into the cabin for Greg and Dylan to get on the VHF (and to make sure they had pants on). We had visitors.

"You guys might be the craziest thing I've ever seen. You need anything?" asked the dreadlocked Dave Carter of the forty-foot sailboat *Beth*. To the four of us, his vessel—eleven feet longer than ours—looked like the lap of luxury.

Dylan responded: "We're trying for an unassisted crossing, and we're not allowed to accept any food."

Dave sailed circles around us. He and a crew of two Belgians and a swimming cat were on a voyage from Jamaica to Bristol via the Azores. "Well, that's fair enough. Sixty days. Are you guys winning?"

"We're racing against two British teams and we're 200 miles up on the first one and 450 on the second one." It felt good after weeks of slugging it out to still be ahead, but the numbers had become almost meaningless to us. With the northeast winds, the truth was that the next few days would be tough. We were about 240 miles from the finish line. "Let's hope it's in the bag," said Dylan.

Beth sailed some more loops and we continued to row, basking in the sun and the warmth of human exchange until they moved on.

—✺—

By 9:00 PM we were 213 miles from the finish line. We'd rowed thirty-three miles east since early morning. If this speed kept up, we would cross the two-hundred-mile barrier and eat another hundred-mile meal. Burch had given us the latest weather forecast earlier that day: eight- to ten-knot west to northwest winds this evening. We could easily travel eastward, and if we tolerated a bit rougher rowing, we could even make a few more miles north, which would be important when the wind turned again. After that, there would be favorable north-by-northwest winds, and it looked stable through August 14. David's email also mentioned a strange, unseasonable high forming just north and due west of Falmouth.

Two hours later, we remained the same 213 miles away from the finish line. Wind had come earlier than expected. Greg had a one-word entry for the logbook: "Fuck." No one wanted to give up an inch to sea anchor, so we rowed through the night. By morning we had lost two miles.

Day 61

Day 60 had come and gone and we gave little thought to the Dutch record that we had failed to beat. How others would quantify our accomplishment was meaning less and less. It was midmorning and Dylan turned on the video camera. "It's day sixty-two? Sixty-one. I'm wasted; I've never been this down in my entire life. I...I'm like up one minute so high and down the next. And when I'm up, I feel like I'm never going to be down again, and when I'm down I feel like we're going to be stuck out here forever." He stumbled over his words like a professional drunk. "This wind is just driving me insane. We've got seven days of food. I mean that's everything. This is crazy.... I don't know what else to do except for just go to sleep and wake up and row, and I'm just rowing because I don't know what else to do, there's no choice. It's...it's...it's awful."

Dylan wore a long-sleeved navy shirt, which made his empty eyes appear a brilliant blue. He'd never wanted to be at home more in his entire life. The finish line was so close that with a shift in the wind, we could be there in a few days. We had rowed 3232 miles, but we could fail in the last 200. Even with all we had been through—the food rationing, the storms, the bodily ailments—we could very well not make it. The prospect was devastating.

Physically Dylan looked better than the rest of us, fuller cheeks and an olive tan, but he had reached rock bottom. Low points of this twenty-month odyssey had come and gone, but this was a new type of low. He was beyond the point of missing family and friends—it was too painful. The voyage was consuming us.

—√√—

Night began to fall and the waves closed the horizon around us. A black-hulled fishing boat with bright lights approached. Thousands of seabirds swarmed the stern, and the smell of fish overpowered us. Dark blue waves the size of SUVs topped with whitecaps crashed against the hull. Three bewildered fishermen looked out at us. With a mix of French, Spanish, and English on the VHF, we managed to convey that we were okay. We were well within the rich fishing grounds of the continental shelf three hundred feet below us. Fishing vessels, with their unpredictable courses, could be added to the bottleneck of the English Channel.

Northeast winds held us in place with the gentle firmness of a parent's hand. We were stonewalled two hundred miles from the finish line at Bishop Rock's meridian. At our fastest it would be a stretch to get to shore by August 14. Greg would not get to see his sister. She'd spent money and time on him. He could not shake the feeling that he'd somehow failed her. Greg had never been so tired. He had distinguished himself with a cast-iron ability not to fall asleep on the oars as well as to wake up and row on demand. Now he was mortal like the rest of us, and in the late night he found himself dipping in and out of consciousness on the oars.

The high that had continued to build was an omega block, a weather phenomenon so rare for this time of year that David Burch himself was amazed by it. A "block," in weatherspeak, is an extremely stable high that can settle in one place for days and even weeks—longer than our food stores. Falmouth, in the center of this pattern, was expecting consistently sunny weather. On the outside of the forming high, we would be forced to fight to get through the increasing northeast winds building a wall around our destination. All we could do was zigzag our way east, waiting for the winds to alter enough to make miles. As of David's latest message, even bigger east winds unrelated to the omega block were also coming in. When they ended, we could have a three-day respite to get close enough to Falmouth to battle through the border of the stable high.

Hundreds of miles behind, there was no way the *Yorkshire Warrior* and the *Commando Joe* could get through the omega block before the high winds on its borders fully formed.

—*∿∿*—

My father and brother would be leaving before we hit land. I wrote to my mother: "I have accepted the fact that I may not see Dad and Doug, but they are in my heart." I felt like Jim Hanssen had wanted me to learn this lesson on the water: I have a chance to know Jim Wood in a way that I had not been able to know him, and I need to make that a priority.

On shore our toil was a dot on screen. Our ARGOS tracking beacon updated the boat's movement minute by minute. Sign of a struggle could only be inferred by a gain or lack of progress of the dot, but the details of our relentless effort were invisible. Rebecca wrote me about Odysseus's struggle to escape angry Poseidon to the safe shores of Phaeacia on his way home to Ithaca.

As I had known and loved Rebecca, I knew she was strong in body and will. As the row across the ocean had extended into its second month, I detected a quiet Penelopean strength in her writing: "He washed up on shore covered in brine, a bit beaten up but he enjoyed the warmth of the land, the warm welcome by the gods and a good night's rest." She was concluding a vignette from the *Odyssey*. "So to you I say, soon you will be to land, this may be your last great trial out there. I pray it is. You have a warm body waiting to hold you, look after you, and love you. I can't wait to see you."

She was not the only one channeling the *Odyssey* at this point. "Keep Ithaca fixed in your minds," the secretary at the Seattle Maritime Academy, where we had done our safety training, texted to us. Inner will had supplanted earthly wants. Every two hours the two men in the cabin came out to replace the men on deck. Two hours later it happened again. I was in awe of my crew and said as much that night in my video diary: "Even in our weakened condition, I can't help but think this is the strongest all four of us have ever been. We are running on empty, and we're drawing strength from places that we didn't know we had." Each time we stepped out of the cabin, we made a choice.

It was almost Day 62. We chose Ithaca.

—◠◠◠—

Chapter 23

A Moment in Time

Day 62

Erinn Hale, our still photographer, stood in line by the Megabus station in London. She clutched her camera—her livelihood— tightly to her chest. It was useless now to dwell upon it, and yet the sick feeling of being violated lingered. All her money, credit cards, and her passport were gone. Thank God the camera and computer had been between her and the wall of the pub booth.

Fourteen months had passed since Erinn had met Greg on a flight from New York to Seattle. She never dreamed that within a year she would be in England, robbed, broke, and without a place to stay in Falmouth. She was now on her way to find a twenty-nine-foot rowboat somewhere off the coast. But she had her camera, and if OAR Northwest continued to row, she was going to get her shot.

—◠◠◠—

By virtue of his very existence, Dylan was not as destroyed as he had claimed the day before. The sun pushed back the night and our red-and-white hull wedged its way east on a cold sunny day. Rowing at one knot, sustained over the next ten days, would cover the remaining two hundred miles. In addition to the unseasonably stable high forming like an invisible wall around Falmouth, an unexplained current had been added to the mix. We made progress for two six-hour segments in the morning and evening, but in the afternoon and middle of the night the tide, if it was tide, seemed

I take a break from the oars for a mug of oatmeal.

to reverse and push the vessel south, sometimes completely halting progress. We thought the incredible semidiurnal tidal flux present in the English Channel might provide an explanation, but Burch was not convinced. Whatever it was, its predictability made it tolerable. Winds continued to be the wild card and thus worth the worry.

—⁓—

Falmouth was cute, bigger than Emily and Rebecca had imagined, but after six days of the stimulation of London, the charming seaside quays quickly became dull. They headed west thirty miles to explore the wind-beaten promontory on the end of Cornwall's Penwith Peninsula, known as Land's End. Cloudless skies let the unfiltered sun shine upon them. The light wind neither cooled their skin from the August heat nor stirred up the water into frothy whitecaps. It was easy to imagine a rowboat making excellent time in these conditions.

To the east, the clear sky disappeared into a haze of clouds, suggesting different conditions beyond the horizon. North, jutting from the promontory on the barren tan rocks, sat a rusty hulk of some long-forgotten fishing boat, many feet above the high tide line—proof of the water's power. Rebecca took a picture. A white signpost marked the location, stating the distance to New York, the top of Scotland, and the Isles of Scilly. In unison, they yelled hellos at the tops of their lungs out into the ocean. Satisfied we had heard them, Rebecca and Emily made their way down to the beach and skipped rocks into the untiring waves.

—⁓—

I sat on deck with my head down to keep the loose, rocking antenna of our broken but not quite busted satellite phone toward the sky. Todd Soliday, the cameraman waiting for our arrival, needed to plan logistics. He and Kathy Minnis, the producer of the documentary team, had been in England for two weeks. All they could do was sit in Falmouth and wait until our journey across the sea would coincide with Todd's camerawork. He gave me directions to hand off the large yellow watertight case with extra cameras to Captain Mark Terry when *Sula* came out to meet us at the finish line.

"Man, it's good to hear you," said Todd. His thick voice betrayed the brevity of our three-month acquaintance. I was touched.

185

"It's good to hear your voice, too." I gave him the boat's party line: "We're ready to be in, but it's not our choice; it's the ocean's." Todd was talking like getting to the finish was a sure thing. I was no longer so sure. "What it comes down to is who's on shore is on shore. Either way, we're going to be in England."

In the past twenty-four hours, Betsy had traveled by train eight hundred miles from the top of Scotland to the end of the line in Penzance to visit a friend. An old Cornish man on the train that afternoon told her that her boyfriend was now rowing into some of the world's strongest tides and currents. As she clicked send on her email to Greg, Betsy wondered if it was a good thing to have mentioned.

—‿‿‿—

One shift a day, often in the middle of the afternoon, seemed impossible to sleep through. Greg lay in the cabin, eyes closed, listening to Pearl Jam's "Leather Man" on the iPod. If the North Atlantic had taught us anything, it was that unpredictability was the rule. It was not against the laws of physics that a westerly wind might decide to blow hard for three days. It just wasn't likely. With less than 10 percent of the distance left to cover, Greg accepted that, like the rest of us, he was exploring unknown territory for his mind, body, and soul. He just wanted to be done. Food would run out in ten days—that was a fact. Greg reluctantly sent a message telling his sister Angie he would not see her on this side of the sea. I knew he felt sad about it, and it irritated me that he just wouldn't admit it.

—‿‿‿—

David Burch put down the phone, took off his glasses, and squeezed the bridge of his nose. Staring at a screen of wind predictions, he was pleased that his weather reports were manifesting themselves, but he was not thrilled to tell the team that more bad wind was coming. They were doing well, given the circumstances, but they remained two hundred miles out at sea. His involvement had become a bit of an obsession, but the thought of backing out never crossed his mind. It was a matter of seamanship. Had he known what he was getting into eight months ago, well, he might have politely shown us the door. But he had not and he would see the team through as best he could. Even a five-day weather report that could change at the last minute was better than nothing at all, wasn't it?

—⁂—

Brad was no longer excited. If his parents or his buddy Chris had been able to change their flights, that would be great. But it was easier on the mind to just imagine his Uncle Peter, who lived in the countryside near Falmouth, as the only family who would be around to see him in. The last of the breakfast packs, with their small ration of sugar, had been eaten this morning. Breakfast would have nothing sweet in it until England. Almost nothing—I was putting Emergen-C packets in my "breakfast" polenta as a sugar substitute. This grossed Brad out to no end, but he found it hard to judge considering he had taken to chewing his toothbrush to compensate for two months of mushy food. We had entered the final act.

Day 63

Erinn arrived in town via train the morning of August 11, her luck much improved. In less than an hour, Erinn had a ride into town, a place to stay, and a job washing dishes at Pepe's Spanish restaurant. She would start that night. Glowing with the turn of events, she dropped off her bag at the hostel and made her way to check in at OAR Northwest's Falmouth headquarters, the Cinnamon Girl Cafe.

One of the very first things David and Marie Spooner had done after their arrival in Falmouth over a week ago was reconnoiter the town for Wi-Fi internet and a suitable cup of coffee. They had found both in the Cinnamon Girl. Fifteen enthusiastic family members and friends had now ensconced themselves in the cafe, drinking lattes and eating organic baked goods while compulsively refreshing the internet map of our location. For hours at a time, they checked for the latest on weather patterns, the water blog, and personal correspondence from the boat. All locals interacting with the group learned why they were in the tiny seaside town that normally attracted more English tourists than American. Our proud parents took any opportunity that presented itself to brag about their brave sons. After a week of their spreading the good news about our impending arrival, the town buzzed with anticipation.

Todd and Kathy were on hand to film the brewing enthusiasm. They loved Falmouth, but each day they were bleeding cash, and there was only so much B-roll they could shoot. If they wanted to stay, they would have to start using some of their own money. For all the forces of obligation pulling them home, Falmouth pulled stronger. This was the prearranged conclusion of what had grown beyond our own adventure to include them all. No one could leave until the finale.

Emily opened up her email in the cafe, hopeful that another message from Dylan might have arrived. Her heart swelled to see the bold lettering of a new message. "I don't know how long you can [stay] in England," he wrote, "but coming out to see us is the most wonderful thing anyone has ever done for me. If we don't make it in before you have to leave, just know that you have already made my life easier by flying halfway across the world." She wrote back: she was happy that she had someone worth flying across an ocean for. Although she rationally accepted the possibility that she might not see him for several more weeks until they were both back in Seattle, she damn well intended to see Dylan on this side of the sea.

Chapter 24

Transition to Land

Dylan and Brad wondered if two people could hallucinate the same smell. Late that night the wind shifted briefly to the north and the rain disappeared. The air flowed over them with the odor of whiskey-pungent peat moss and the sharp smell of manure. This was distinct from the reek of beach at low tide—it was the comforting tang of a fecund inland pasture. The GPS assured us that the closest landmass remained Ireland. Dylan tentatively broached the subject, much to Brad's relief that he was not going crazy. For ten glorious minutes, until the wind shifted back to rain, they basked in the invisible evidence of terra firma.

Greg and I woke at the five-minute call. Groggily assuming our posts, we prepared for the darkest shift of the night, listening passively as Brad and Dylan described the experience with exuberance. The smell had long since passed, but they wished us another wind shift so we might also bask in the rich smell of dirt. We had entered a transitioning world—not land, but no longer completely open ocean. Mizen Head, the southwesternmost tip of County Cork, was now 130 miles to our north. With a good wind it was still conceivable we could finish on August 15, the twenty-first anniversary of my father's death.

In Sligo my mother and father had lived on Rosses Point in a white cottage in Ballyweelin, across the bay from Knocknarea. Less than an eighth of a mile down the point, in a converted schoolhouse known as The Anchorage, lived my father's parents, Stan and Jeanne. My father, along with his older sister Peggy and younger brother Eric, had lived in this house when the family had moved

Me and my first dad, Jim Hanssen, on the beaches in Portugal

In a hammock with my new dad in Las Cruces, New Mexico.
It seemed too soon to everyone but me.

from Chicago. My grandfather had never insisted his children follow him into the Hanson Scales business, but he was delighted to have them. Uncle Eric joined the business in 1979 and my father followed soon after. With him he brought his new wife, my mother Eve.

Eve had never lived outside of Mobile, Alabama. Ireland's rugged and cold, windswept west coast was a shock after the subtropical climate she had grown up in—only the abundance of green was familiar. Stan and Jeanne loved my mother from the start. In 1982, the year I was born, my grandparents exchanged the emerald of Ireland for expansive blue skies in Las Cruces, New Mexico, where they started another scale business. Uncle Eric joined them, as did Hugo Fischer, one of the family's oldest friends from Chicago. My father stayed in Europe to head the factories in England, Ireland, and France. A year later we moved from Sligo to the English village of Pebworth, to a house known as High Roost.

—⁓—

When my father died at home on August 15, 1985, neighbors came as they saw the ambulance lights, asking my mother whom they could call. Vacillating between shock and grief, Eve could not bring herself to call Stan and Jeanne and tell them that their son was dead. Her mother, Helen, four thousand miles away in Mobile, seemed the only choice. Helen knew from my mother's tone someone had died. "Is it Jim or Jordan?" she'd asked. Little could be done to comfort her daughter. She called Becky, my mother's sister, and began the tragic phone chain.

Becky had just married Hugo Fischer earlier that summer in Las Cruces. My father had given Becky away at their wedding. Hugo, my dad, and Uncle Eric had been childhood friends, and it fell to Hugo to tell the rest of the family of Jim's death. Within twenty-four hours Stan, Jeanne, Eric, Peggy, and Helen arrived in Pebworth.

My father's body was autopsied. His lungs were scarred from asthma. The family's traditions at a time of death have come down from my Grandmother Jeanne's father, my great-grandfather Eugene "Pops" Bergman. According to my grandmother, Pops was the first to make an "A" in anatomy at the University of Washington. Intelligent, analytical, and irreligious, he was no atheist. Pops saw no reason for science to be at odds either with his spiritual belief in an afterlife or with his own power of clairvoyance. He made many predictions, including the family's move to Ireland from Chicago long before it had become a consideration, going as far as to pick the latitude and longitude of where they would live on Rosses Point. Pops viewed the body as vessel. He believed that when someone started to die, the spirits of their relatives gather to guide the soul from the physical world into the next. The earthly remains lose any connection to the person. If death is unexpected, there is no time to gather and the soul lacks guidance for this transition. By implication, it meant my father's soul had not yet made it to the next world. Death was private to Pops, and he wanted no one to say rites over his body or even to conduct a service in his honor. When he died seventeen years before my father, his wish was respected. My grandmother believed in Pops's order of things and passed down this concept of spirituality to the family.

It's doubtful Jim Hanssen spent any more time than the average thirty-two-year-old contemplating mortality on the morning of his death. Asthma had been a fact of his life. In turn, the plastic receptacle that held his ashes could hardly be called an urn, but its practicality fit our traditions.

Knocknarea is wreathed in dark heather and green grass. Under the clouds it seems almost black. On its eastern slope, gray rock has been pulled up from the soil to make low stone walls that fence the land into uneven fields where sheep, cows, and horses graze. From a distance, it looks like an overturned warrior's shield. This hill-upon-the-hill is a Neolithic cairn where the Warrior Queen Maeve is alleged to have been buried upright—facing her enemies in the Kingdom of Ulster to the north. The broad thousand-foot mountain sits on a peninsula inside a shallow bay. Just west is the North Atlantic. Across the bay is Rosses Point, where my dad spent his formative high school years looking out at this mountain. Climbing it was one of the first things he, Eric, and Peggy did whenever they came back to Ireland. Shortly after my birth, my father told my mother that Knocknarea was where he wanted his ashes scattered.

―◈―

The weather was good when the family reached Sligo, and we wasted no time in starting out on the trail of rock, mud, and grass. This is my first memory after his death. I held my mom's hand for the first few hundred yards, then let go and climbed the rest of Knocknarea without help. Seven of us stood on the ancient cairn with no priest to lead us in our grief. Hanssens did not typically pray; if they did, it was silent. My grandparents handed the ashes to my mom to scatter. After having a son of her own, my mother felt it was not her place, but Stan and Jeannie insisted. The wind blew the ashes west across the cairn and toward the sea. After a light rain my father's mortal remains would soak into the earth from which they had come. Nothing was said. Just six adults lost in silent grief and a three-year-old boy. I have no recollection of how I felt at the time.

My grandmother Jeanne saw God in the orchestration of the abandoned summit, the brief blue sky, and the east wind. It was nature: good, clean, and pure. Many years before, when Pops was very ill, he had told her of a vision of having a meeting on top of the mountain. She smiled when she remembered this. Pops was meeting his grandson. Too soon for her liking, but she knew Jimmy was in good company. The family had told no one they were coming to Sligo, but when we arrived that evening so many flowers had been sent that they had to store them in the bathtub.

In the days after his death, over sixty telegrams from businessmen in a dozen countries had arrived at the factory in Sligo. In a month, this number would grow to more than 170 from twenty-six countries on six continents in a half dozen languages. They paint a composite portrait as the people my father worked with perceived him. Summed up, he was a gentleman in the word's purest definition. Who exactly Jim Hanssen was is impossible for me to know. Perhaps he worked too hard, and perhaps my mother was sometimes lonely. He could be nervous and fidgety and possibly so eager to take care of my mother that she may not have had as much room to grow as she would have liked when they were together. For the rest of the portrait I could look at what I do not like in myself. I am told I am in many ways like Jim Hanssen, but I'd rather claim those imperfections as my own.

Day 63

Out on the ocean, so close to Ireland, I felt the pilgrim's anticipation that preceded earlier visits to Knocknarea. If we could row a little less than fifty miles a day over the next four days, I could cross the finish line on August 15 and mark that day with something else besides his death.

Dylan smiling in spite of the uneasy feeling of resting on the sea anchor

Chapter 25

—–ⱳⱳ–—

A Mile Is Better Than
None at All

*When one rows, it is not the rowing which moves the ship:
rowing is only a magical ceremony by means of which one
compels a demon to move the ship.*

—Friedrich Nietzsche

Day 64

I fed the thick, yellow nylon rope of the sea anchor through my fingers. Half-evaporated sea salt gave it a slimy texture. The daily shift in current and unfavorable wind pulled the submerged parachute away from the boat. With this predictable semidiurnal current, progress would be impossible for several hours out of every day. Shifting the paradigm from acquiescence to strategy made the prospect of forced rest more manageable.

It was August 12. David Burch was still adamant we stay north. Having this fifty-nautical-mile-long virtual gate as the finish line changed the game. Many previous ocean rows on the North Atlantic declared their stated finish goal to be the meridian of Bishop Rock. This opens up a rather loose and large target area that technically meant a boat could cross anywhere roughly 160 miles north of the rock before hitting Ireland and about 440 miles south of it before hitting Spain. Such a wide finish line would have allowed us to take advantage of more diverse wind patterns. A brisk north-by-northeast wind shut us down as we headed in the direction of the virtual gate, still northeast of us. However, this same wind would allow for southeast progress. Had an open-ended finish line been our strategy from the start, we could have saved perhaps a week or more letting the wind decide our heading.

Our current latitude vacillated ten to fifteen miles north of the bottom of the gate. Two days hence, the weather window predicted west-by-southwest wind for three straight days. This would be perfect—blowing us firmly east and slightly north, where we had the greatest margin for error. For now, five-foot waves and fifteen knots of wind were coming out of the northeast. We could make progress southeast in this weather, but at the cost of our cushion above the bottom of the gate. When the west wind picked up, we would have to fight our way north perpendicular to the west by southwest wind to get up and around the finish gate. While we fought the strong wind, it would provide an advantage for our opponents, the *Yorkshire Warrior* and the *Commando Joe*, who were at this point roughly two hundred and four hundred miles, respectively, behind us. We had given little thought to them since early August, as food concerns loomed and our lead extended. Recklessness could make this a much closer race, and without the fifty-five-day record to pursue, it was better to play it safe.

So we waited, north of the bottom of the gate and 156 miles west of it. Greg updated Dylan and Brad about our decision to sit. It would take roughly six hours for the current to shift again if it continued its regular course. Eating was out of the question but sleep was not. Greg and I posted a three-hour watch. We pulled our hoods over knit caps and tightened each strap on our foul weather gear to retain maximum warmth. Then we folded our bodies between the twenty-two-inch-wide tracks. Sleep eluded us, yet we found restful tranquility in the rocking waves. Three hours later, our shift was up and we headed below.

I woke to the sound of oars pulling us north of east. At 10:00 PM we were back on sea anchor. We had rowed seventeen out of twenty-four hours and made eleven miles east. Each pair slept in shifts on deck again. And like the night before it was tolerable.

Day 65

After nearly eight hours on sea anchor that morning, we had finally started moving when our steering system broke after three thousand miles of continuous use. It was a simple design, basically the marriage of sailing hardware and a foot steering system common in racing shells without coxswains. A small aluminum car ran on an aluminum rail horizontally on the plate where the bowman put his feet. Low-stretch sailing line ran from either side of the stainless steel hooks screwed into the car, to pulleys on the side of the boat, to the rudder. The right foot could pivot and a steel bar ran from the toe to the top of the car, where it was attached with polymer twine.

The stainless steel screw that held one of the stainless steel loops directly onto the aluminum car had fallen out. Disparity in the number of electrons in the different metals, combined with conductive saltwater, caused the stainless steel screw to corrode the aluminum thread through a process called electrolysis. We had a spare; Greg held the steering line in place while I made the fix. I noticed our hands, pale and white at the outset of this voyage, had become leathery brown from constant exposure, despite the gloves that we sometimes wore. Our fingers had grown skinny and our palms were covered with hard yellow calluses. The steel wrench and screwdriver had been stored in a canvas tool bag in the bow compartment. They had been relatively protected from the environment but had almost rusted into uselessness. Everything aged faster on the water.

North-by-northeast wind continued to blow. On the very edge of the horizon, between the gray clouds and grayer water, this dreary world cracked open just enough to reveal a brilliant ring of yellow and orange around the boat, suggesting the existence of the sun. Small whitecaps danced on top of large swells from the east. We rowed in slow motion 150 miles from the finish. According to Burch, this was a waiting day. There was a light at the end of the tunnel. We were to try to make east while trying to stay north of the line.

Each stroke felt like we were building up pressure, like eventually the tether holding us back would snap and we would fly across the line. Wind would come from the west for the next two days, but on the third day, a new wind would come into play as a low moved over us from the north. Low pressure would invite southeast winds of currently inestimable velocity to our estimated location to fill this void. Burch assured us that in order to get to land, the next forty-eight hours were absolutely critical. He instructed us to get east. "There will be no rest for about five days," he explained, but then "it's party time."

Since the last shift change, there had been little spoken of the decision to no longer alternate rowers. Every four days, for two months, we had committed to this rotation. It had kept the crew homogeneous. Not rotating seemed a way to exacerbate differences and build separate identities, which could do no good if a situation occurred where each distinct team—loyal to each other and not the boat—split us into factions. Mixing it up forced everyone to come to terms with each other. Four days seemed to be the sweet spot between becoming just sick enough of someone's proximity to look forward to a new person, and not long enough to build up lasting animosity.

However, the truth was that Greg had reached the end of his patience with Brad. The combinations of Greg and myself plus Dylan and Brad led to the least amount of conflict. On the fifth day of rowing together, each pair had begun to create distinct personalities.

Our latest estimate on our earliest possible landfall was now on August 18. I had to let go of finishing on August 15, the anniversary of my father's death. At first I wondered what I had done wrong. What God would take my father and not allow me this homage? But then it didn't matter at all, because we were still a tiny boat in a great big sea. Greg tried to use the satellite phone to reach shore and, he hoped, Angie. She was leaving Falmouth tomorrow, and he wanted to thank her for coming anyway. He tried several times, but the number would not go through. I emailed Rebecca that morning. She would be in Ireland until August 15, before returning to Falmouth. Our rowing pace in the upcoming weather would determine whether I would see her in Falmouth or a month later back in Seattle.

Dylan felt like we'd spent a week trying to row fifty miles. Actually it was just over a hundred miles; we finally celebrated inching over the longitude 10° west into single digits toward the zero-degree Greenwich Meridian. Our trip had started in New York at 74° west. In twelve hours we had made ten miles east, at the cost of eight miles south toward the bottom of the gate. Crossing this line meant we were just over 3.5° west of Bishop Rock meridian. It was a satisfying milestone.

An hour later, we were back on sea anchor 140 miles from the finish. Greg wondered if the world was running out of east wind.

Greg taking a break mid-shift (Erinn J. Hale)

—◆◆◆—

Dream Boat

Day 66

In the night Dylan dreamed the four of us had been traveling and become lost. We were mountain biking in Humboldt, Dylan's home county in California. We followed a trail he knew. Greg was so fast that the rest of us couldn't keep up. Everyone was impressed. We ended up by a river, where a museum was charging seven dollars to go into the river. OAR Northwest was not going to pay twenty-eight dollars, so we broke out our boat (which we'd somehow been carrying) and proceeded to get in and row. In his dream I steered the rudder in the back. As we rowed away from the museum, Dylan saw a father and his son standing onshore. The dad put his hand on the kid's shoulder, and pointed to us and said, 'Look, son. It's OAR Northwest.' As we rowed away, four kids floated along behind us in inner tubes with flame-throwers scorching the sides of the riverbank. With that image, Dylan woke up.

"That's kick-ass," said Greg.

"It's been the highlight of my day so far." Dylan's satisfaction was evident. Sea anchor had lasted till 9:30 PM the night before, giving the team another five hours of unwanted rest. Perhaps the extra sleep accounted for the increasingly strange and transparent dreams we were having.

Of the last thirty-one hours, we'd spent twelve on sea anchor. In the nineteen hours on oar, we made ten miles east at the sacrifice of eight miles south. With gains like this, we would end up in France.

But since our last log entry, seven hours had passed and we had made a staggering twenty-five miles east. Had we kept up this rate for seven days, we would have made almost six hundred miles and long been on shore.

Greg did some calculations in the logbook. Over the past two weeks we had rowed 380 miles. Our previous slowest five-hundred-mile segment had taken thirteen days. We could have strolled for ten hours a day, enjoyed a leisurely morning and evening plus eight hours of sleep for two weeks and gone about the same distance that we had after plugging away on the oars twenty-four hours a day. Granted, we hauled a boat that weighed twenty-four hundred pounds (down from thirty-four hundred), but it didn't make our sluggishness easier to accept.

Today the miles dropped behind our wake, but a half day's good progress was not enough to excite us. The low front skirting on the edge of the larger omega block had passed directly over us, and we rowed through relatively light and irregular winds while the *Yorkshire Warrior* and the *Commando Joe* battled thirty-five-knot winds from the north on the edge of the low. The good breeze Burch had promised proved elusive, causing him to coin the aphorism that "the good wind is always tomorrow." Our best heading was now directly for the center of the finish line.

Greg tried again to reach his parents and Angie on the sat phone. Still no luck, although he did receive a message they sent from the airport as they had waited for Angie's plane. There had been an averted terrorist plot on August 10 to blow up as many as ten planes over the Atlantic—all flight traffic out of England had been stopped or delayed. Angie would be on the first flight to Seattle since the scare. This close to land, airplane traffic had become quite frequent. I imagined them falling from the sky and distantly grasped the significance of the averted tragedy. All I could worry about was the wind.

Along with all the other downloaded emails was an unexpected note from Brad's parents. Brad had kept his head in the boat better than anyone, a task made easier by his lack of a sweetheart and his laconic parents. He seemed less worse for wear because of this. His parents remained at his uncle's cottage outside of town, writing him while a herd of cows was taken into Uncle Peter's field to graze. Their sparse correspondence had the knack of showing up exactly when Brad needed it. Brad was not particularly religious, but a prayer they had found from the Celtic Irish Saint Columba, urging Jesus to be with us in the "troughs of waves, on the crest of billows" did not go unappreciated.

I needed to write several emails that day, whose subject matter soured my mood in spite of the best progress we had experienced in more than a week. Fog filled my brain, and each simple movement took deliberate action as I wrote Jim Wood and my brother: "Two weeks to move 380 miles. This has been the challenge. The hardest part? Being apart from you guys." The only thing I can rely on, I explained, is nature's unpredictability. I had accepted that I probably would not see Jim and Douglas in Falmouth, a bitter pill to swallow. I told them: "If anything, this experience has taught me that I need to spend more time with you two. If it took this to teach me that, then all is well."

Our fingernails had developed ridges on them from malnutrition. The boat smelled horrible—wet must mixed with fiberglass, and in some hatches where we kept our garbage and food, the acrid smell of rot. I wrote my mom: "Thank you for staying and being a constant. I so look forward to spending time with you. Pray for good wind." Although she had taken about two months to accept that I was serious about rowing the ocean, she had never called me or this obsession crazy, and I knew she would remain in Falmouth until I was safe on shore.

Days earlier, it had seemed like Rebecca and I would have time to walk quayside streets in Falmouth hand in hand. But August 21 was six days away, and one more week would keep me from her. I wrote to her: "I am sorry I am not on shore. Can you forgive me?" She had come to see the end. She had come for me. "I love you," I typed. "I hope to see you in England, but no matter what, I will see you soon."

———

Throughout the day we had made a consistent two knots, sometimes achieving between three and five, as the current turned in our favor. By midnight we had less than one hundred miles to go.

Out of New York we had nearly covered this distance in a single day. I felt like the entire crew was on a balance beam with one person always falling off. The three balanced members would reach out and steady the fourth, and another would start to fall. How long could we keep this up?

PART SIX

*Dylan gets out on deck to continue
the endless cycle of rowing and sleeping.*
(Erinn J. Hale)

—∿∿—

Chapter 27

Dirty Thirty

Day 67

By morning the trip odometer stated that we had rowed 3466 miles since leaving New York. On a perfect course, unmolested by winds and current, this would have put us through the east end of the English Channel. Instead, we surfed optimistically eighty-four miles west of the finish line.

Dylan's voice sounded strong as he explained the situation on the sat phone to our documentary team, Todd and Kathy. "It's supposed to be dead today and light from the west, then picking up from the south tomorrow," he said. "With good wind for the next two days, we'll be able to push across no matter what." They wanted to know if we would row to shore and complete the journey in Falmouth by oar power alone, while we knew we had to consider the food situation at that point. "Finish line first," Dylan told them, "then we'll see what happens."

A discussion arose about an alternate landing spot closer than the seventy miles to Falmouth. The two likeliest places were the Isles of Scilly themselves, thirty miles north of the center of the finish line, and Penzance, fifty miles from the same spot. David Burch struck both of these ideas down. First, he explained, this was a decision we could put off until we crossed the line. Second, he didn't believe the tides in the alternate places would be as safe as they would be in Falmouth. Third, our stated destination was Falmouth, and it was just good seamanship to end up where you said you would. We had some time to make these decisions. For simplicity's sake, Dylan told the filmmakers it was a tow or a row into Falmouth. That meant Todd had to be in the Isles of Scilly in twenty-four hours if he was going to find us on the water to film the finish.

Mother Nature was gunning for a showdown. The day before's oddly sunny and warm low-pressure zone yielded to sopping drops of rain and a plunge in temperature. Wind whipped counterclockwise, creating strong unfavorable winds fifty miles ahead of and behind us. At our location, in the center, the wind was weaker but volatile. According to David, all the weather maps displayed something different. His advice in this crapshoot was to run as fast as possible to the center of the finish gate with no more sacrifices south.

———

Rebecca returned to Falmouth from Ireland and was back at the Cinnamon Girl Cafe. The scuttlebutt was that our boat would be getting a tow from the finish line to get us on shore faster. Concerned at this development, she wrote to me: "Do what the four of you need to do. Don't listen to people here, don't listen to me. Do what you need to do for yourself. This is your life and no one else's, so live it. Listen to your heart, to your Dad, to God, and take it from there!"

Rarely did she write with such emotion. Getting a tow the last seventy miles from the finish gate to Falmouth was never how we wanted to end it. Rebecca was 160 miles away. She would be leaving in just five days. Choosing to get a tow would almost guarantee that I would see her, but with a few words she had erased any weakness that might influence how I voted for us to finish.

———

The evening before, Greg and I had entertained ourselves by exchanging yarns from our childhood, specifying that the experiences must have occurred between the ages of five and eleven. The meandering path of the two-month conversation that filled the hours on oars now required specific stipulations and provisos to ensure the chat covered new ground. A common character emerged in the tales I spun for Greg. Story after story featured my stepfather. Ski trips complete with doughnut continental breakfasts, heated swimming pools, an airplane ride in a Cessna above the desert and over my mom's house, where she waved up at us from the garden. Jim had let me hold the controls while he took a picture of her from the air, which he later printed out in an eight-by-eleven format. I had never seen a photo that big.

When I nearly blew off my hand after a particularly enthusiastic Fourth of July party, Jim bandaged me up. He also called me out on a lie when I insisted that the celebratory ordinance had exploded without provocation. Without him, I would not have had two parents tell me on a sunny late-winter day that I would have a brother coming that fall.

Jim Wood had not acquired the responsibility of fatherhood in the typical way. He was never entirely sure he wanted kids. My mother, the woman he fell in love with, happened to have a five-year-old. Granted, the two of us came as a pair, and I don't think my mom would have married another man not willing to be as much a father to me as a husband to her. This meant he had made a conscious choice to be both. Jim himself was the youngest of six children and less than a year old when a drunk driver killed his mother Betty. His father Roy later married the woman I came to know as my Grandma Evie. She had been widowed and had two children of her own. She and Roy had two more children, making a grand total of ten kids.

There are risks living with ghosts. Death enshrines everyone, especially those who die young. Jim Wood knew little of my father's flaws, and as confident as he appeared, he sometimes wondered how he measured up to Jim Hanssen as a father. He never adopted me, although he offered. This was my mother's choice, out of empathy for my grandparents. I was what was left of their son, and for that reason I would stay a Hanssen. Consciously they made sure that I would never forget Jim Hanssen. The walls and shelves of family photos included both men.

It is the craftsmanship in the construction of my family that baffles me. I do not see the seams where even I think there should be some. I typed a quick email to Jim Wood, thanking him for choosing to be my father. I hoped he would be able to read my message before boarding his flight.

—ᴧᴧᴧ—

Erinn was worried about how she would get on the water for her shots. Todd and Kathy were looking into their own ride to the finish gate, and it was doubtful Erinn would be able to find space on whatever craft they found. For the next few hours it didn't matter. A dreamy-looking Welshman had asked her out to eat at the only Chinese restaurant in town. She was enjoying herself immensely at the Lucky Dragon when a short, familiar-looking man entered the restaurant.

It was Stewart, part of the crew from the *Sula*. She stormed over to him and demanded to know why he wasn't out on the water watching us. He explained the less-than-seaworthy nature of *Sula* and his plans to travel to France the next day to secure another boat to meet the *Yorkshire Warrior* and the *Commando Joe*. Meanwhile, Captain Mark Terry was busy rustling up some crew for the rigid inflatable boat (RIB) to meet OAR Northwest on the finish line. This gave Erinn an idea.

—⁓—

Greg and I came on the oars as the horizon faded from gray. In fifteen minutes, the sky was a starless, inky black, and a tempest unleashed itself. A west wind of over thirty knots pulled up the waves into ten-foot and then fifteen-foot swells. Torrential rain, unlike any we had encountered since the pregnant drops of the Gulf Stream, hammered us so heavily that we rowed by Braille. Bodies swung left and right, and the bright orange displays of the compass and GPS receiver overwhelmed my eyes to the point of vertigo. The white noise of a billion slamming drops overwhelmed conversation. Swells rolled over gunwales pouring onto the deck up to our waists. The scuppers struggled to empty the hundreds of pounds of extra weight. Out of the darkness a wave threw enough water over the side to knock me off my seat. My legs flew up over my head as I landed hard between the tracks and the gunwale. Struggling to get back to my post, I caught another wave that pushed my torso out over the gunwale before putting me on the deck.

"Are you okay?" yelled Greg, unable to let go of the steering system or the oars in the waves.

I checked my body for injury—nothing but new bruises. I began an unhinged chuckle, thankful for the nylon webbing that served as my umbilical cord between the boat and the stainless steel rings on my life vest. "I'm just going to lie here for a bit," I replied. After a few deep breaths I cautiously resumed my seat. Seven miles rolled by in ninety minutes. Then the wind shifted to the northwest and dropped to fifteen knots. We had fifty-one miles to go.

―――――

Old nautical tchotchkes crowded the smoke-stained wood paneling and low ceilings that would have felt overdone outside of Falmouth, and yet The Chain Locker seemed to maintain its credibility with the local mariners. The hostel crew tagged along, and what Erinn had planned as a quiet meeting with Mark to discuss getting on the boat turned into the loudest crowd in the pub that night. Mark sized up Erinn. He figured he had enough room for her and his two crewmen. Mark would meet her quayside at 8:00 AM. They raised their glasses to seal the agreement.

Day 68

Greg and I made nearly eight miles in the two-hour madness. Brad and Dylan had come on deck after the wind changed direction. By the middle of their shift our consistent current shifted brutally, reducing our speed by a factor of four. By the time Greg and I woke up for the earliest of the morning shifts, Dylan and Brad had only gained a frustrating two miles.

Erinn waited down by the quay. It was 8:30 AM when Mark's truck careered in behind her after he had run around Cornwall gathering gear. Erinn stepped into the eighteen-foot open RIB. It looked small for a craft that would transport them over the open ocean. Taking a deep breath, she stepped onto the deck. A crewman helped her into a dry suit and rubber boots. She would appreciate the gear after they reached the edge of the harbor and Mark slammed the throttle forward, unleashing the two 150-horsepower engines. In seconds the RIB leaped to forty-five knots.

About an hour later, at a small airport outside Penzance, Todd and Rebecca got on a small twin-engine airplane for the twenty-minute flight to the Isles of Scilly airport on St. Mary's. Kathy would stay behind in Falmouth and continue to run logistics and carry on her job of corralling the family and shooting B-roll. The boat was making incredible time to the finish gate. It would be a close call, and they still had to secure some sort of craft to take them from St. Mary's out to the finish line.

Around noon, I lay in the back cabin staring at sixty-seven days of hash marks. I had hated it when Dylan began this system, but now he could not be bothered and I was the one to ink in the sixty-eighth day. Twenty months of work was coming to an end. The finish line and sighting land, Falmouth, and family were close to becoming reality. Using the flip screen of the video camera as a mirror, I looked into my eyes. They were deep and dark. Beneath the luxuriant beard, I imagined sickly gauntness. Rowing across the Atlantic was probably the unhealthiest thing we had ever done.

Eighty miles east of us, the RIB galloped over large swells. The roar of the engine increased its pitch each time the RIB leaped over a wave. Dark and ominous clouds gathered in the distance in what had to be our direction. Around 1:00 PM, we reached the farthest east we would make that day. The current and wind combined to stall us just under thirty miles from the finish line and around a hundred miles from Falmouth. Dylan and Brad had just gotten off the phone with David Burch. More wind was coming from the north by northeast. There would be no crossing today, but his most dire prediction put us across the finish line in no less than thirty hours, or 6:00 PM the next day.

As the afternoon waned, the wind began to blow strong from the northeast, and we began going backward. Current that had allowed us to take twenty miles in the morning shifted again. We chose to row the treadmill. Losing a quarter mile every hour was better than the mile per hour we would lose on sea anchor. It was like picking at an infected wound.

We had recounted the food two days before, to squeeze out seven days. Rations had shrunk to the smallest we had experienced. Crossing the finish line was not what worried Greg. There was enough food for that. It was the mainland-to-mainland record that had become increasingly important to all of us. Crossing the line would win the race and make us the first native-born Americans to row the North Atlantic. With enough food it would have been a breeze even if we took those miles inch by inch.

But we didn't have enough food. Brad's mistake had happened months ago, but it infuriated Greg as if it had happened yesterday. He could imagine half a dozen people he'd rather have on this boat than Brad. But he also knew that never had he worked with anyone this intensely for so long. For more than two months we had lived and worked on a twenty-nine-foot boat in the middle of the ocean. Now we were thirty miles from finishing a thirty-two-hundred-mile race. The four of us had trusted each other to keep watch while the others slept.

A dark front of high clouds covering the southeastern half of the sea moved menacingly toward us. To port it remained clear, with the start of an orange ember of sunset. Greg and I rowed northeast, fighting to keep from getting blown south. The GPS receiver displayed the gloomy truth that we had been blown around a two-square-mile block of ocean for twelve hours. Into the forbidding cloudscape red and green lights approached out of the darkness. Seeing both port and starboard lights on the big container ship meant it was directly on course for our position.

Greg called to Brad and Dylan to make sure the radar responder and running lights were on. He asked for the VHF and called channel 16. "Large ship to the southwest of us, we are a rowboat two to three miles off your bow, do you copy?" Nothing. We couldn't tell if it was a freighter or a tanker. Referring to ships as "large" was relative: everything was bigger than us. On the smoothest, clearest day, the farthest out we could see a freighter and its eighty-foot bridge was about twelve miles. It had become considerably rougher in the last half hour, and this ship had come out of the darkest portion of the clouds. When we sighted it, it was perhaps four to five miles off. At a speed of around twenty knots, it would cover that distance in less than twelve minutes.

Greg had been hailing the ship for at least three or four minutes without any response, and the red and green lights still loomed. By this time Dylan and Brad had been roused from sleep, and Dylan was looking out the back hatch with increasing concern at the metal leviathan's approach. Greg kept calling on the radio, switching from emergency channel 16 to the bridge-to-bridge channel and back again, to no avail.

As it approached in the twilight, the hull was at its least visible, and the many lights that outlined the ship were still not powerful enough to overpower the setting sun. We could not pick a side with any confidence, and the last thing we wanted to do was to row directly into the ship's path. Waves were coming from the north and the winds from the east boxed us in, creating an awkward position from which the only direction we could go with any swiftness and control was directly toward the bow of the oncoming ship. Going toward starboard or port of the approaching ship would take us uncomfortably close. Obviously they had the right of way, and we were not keen to play chicken with a freighter. Both invisible and slow, we were left with little choice.

Seconds turned to minutes, and the ship loomed larger. I swore we had a protocol for this but could not think through the molasses of exhaustion. Then it hit me. "Where are the flares?" I exclaimed.

Greg looked at me from across the deck, eyes wide. "That is a great idea!" I sorted through the dry bags until I found the one full of foot-long cylinders. Both the white and red parachute flares were yellow with red lettering, hard to read in the dimming light. I picked one.

"Can I shoot it?" asked Greg. This seemed like a perfectly reasonable request in the face of several hundred thousand tons of steel bearing down on us, so I handed it to him. I stared back to the approaching ship. Greg passed the VHF handset to Brad, who continued calling as he brought the flare up to the navigation light to read the directions.

Greg held the flare above his head, looked away, and pulled the tab. There was a pause before a hiss and a puff of smoke and light filled the boat. The rocket propelled itself a thousand feet before its slow parachute descent to the sea. Greg swayed drunkenly, staring at the light with a dazed look before focusing again on the ship. It was less than a mile away. We gazed, transfixed, on the massive freighter still steaming forward at twenty knots. I doubted we could get another flare in the air in time for the ship's crew to do anything about it.

Finally the skyscraper-sized hunk of steel began to list hard starboard before the blue broadside, an eighth of a mile long, finally revealed itself.

"Don't worry, Rowboat, we see you," said a disembodied voice with a French accent.

"He is altering course to starboard," said Brad, with great relief.

We stared in silence, in shock. The freighter's hull blended into the sea and its name was easy to read at this distance. At 643 feet the *CGM Matisse* was pretty big; by volume it could hold 867 of our boats.

The voice crackled on the radio. "It's okay. For your information, we don't see you on our radar; we saw your light. Have a nice day."

Uneasy laughter rippled through the boat. A seventy-dollar flare had altered the massive ship from its course. Three-and-a-half minutes after making its turn, it was well past us. I asked Brad and Dylan to shut the hatches against the coming wake, and Greg and I returned to rowing. The *CGM Matisse* would pass Falmouth in the next six hours.

—ᴡᴡ—

Still at Sea

Erinn and the gang arrived at the island of St. Mary's cold and curious. Where were the rowers? They found some Wi-Fi to poach outside a deli next to the harbor. The *James Robert Hanssen* had moved backward. Mark had a friend in town a few cobblestones away from the local pub. It looked like "the guys" would be arriving late the next day, so he and Erinn settled into some dry clothes and warm beer at the pub to wait.

—ᴡᴡ—

The adrenaline of the near collision had passed, and my thoughts moved toward the real fear of what could have happened—might still happen. Greg pulled his oars in suddenly and quit rowing. I thought he might have to pee, but he did not move. "Are you okay?"

"I don't know," he replied.

If he needed some time, that was fine. I rowed on for several minutes. "Greg, I don't know if I should talk to you or leave you be."

"I don't know," he said.

This was not the Greg I was used to. I had never seen him act as anything but a hard-nosed optimist. I wasn't sure what else to say, so I kept silent. If he needed to talk, I would be right behind him. I kept rowing.

"I planned on quitting," he finally said. "Twice."

"When?" I asked.

"In the summer, and then in the fall."

Brad sits on the bow as we roll into Falmouth. (Erinn J. Hale)

I had no idea why he was telling me this now, and it was kind of breaking my heart. "I'm glad you didn't."

"I felt you guys could handle it," he said. "The whole thing seemed like too much work."

"Why did you stick around?" I asked. Without him, I doubted we would have made it to New York.

"I wanted it." He picked up the oars again, and we rowed on, going nowhere, with the wind howling louder. By the time Dylan and Brad came on deck, it was clear we needed to go on sea anchor. I slept hard and thought I heard thunder.

Day 69

Dylan tapped on the smoky gray hatch. "Time to wake up, guys. Time to row," he said. I felt like I had not moved in days. I cracked the hatch. Dylan had let us sleep for about three hours.

Greg and I stiffly put on rain gear and walked into purgatory. Pillows of clouds still pregnant with water floated toward the south and west. The sun brought light, but the orb itself was not yet visible, and the sea looked like oiled steel. Toward the east, the clouds gathered like clumps of fine pink cotton. We straddled night and day. Lightning still flashed silently deep into the rapidly receding night.

Brad was sleeping in the cramped front cabin. Dylan wore his dry suit double-layered with his foul-weather jacket, his headlamp and life vest—all firmly secured with the lifeline. He began to pull in the sea anchor.

"The finish line is thirty miles away," said Greg, staring into the distance. "It's so close I can taste it."

The current was drifting more in our favor, and the wind had lightened up a bit. It was time to row. I grabbed an oar and placed it in the oarlock as Dylan began to relate the night's adventure.

Brad had taken the front cabin while Dylan sat on deck wrapped in a tarp with his back to the wind. When the storm came from behind us, he pulled the meager shelter over his head. Rain fell in sheets so thick that they obscured the horizon, but not hard enough to blur the lights of ships streaming past us. Dylan had counted at least four at one time.

"At one point I could even do my crossword, then lightning hit the water.... " He gestured about a hundred feet off the boat. "Like, right there." No time separated the flash or the thunder, and the blast had physically shaken Dylan's body. He was the most scared he had been the entire crossing.

"Why didn't you come in the cabin when it got that bad?" I asked.

He hadn't wanted to interrupt our sleep. "And I was happy doing the crossword," Dylan said. "Besides, I passed out the last forty-five minutes." I couldn't tell if he was joking or slightly manic. His effort seemed superhuman. I desperately wanted to be superhuman for my crew too.

—⁓—

Greg and I rowed at a dismal half knot. Last evening haunted me. Our near miss with the _CGM Matisse_ had shown me that we were reacting too slowly. No one had the energy to assess danger and act swiftly. There was a protocol. That was why we had flares. We had discussed it dozens of times. We should have reacted faster. Ship traffic would continue to increase. The only way we could possibly respond faster was to eat more food.

It was time to discuss rations again. If that meant we had to get a tow, then that was too bad. If I could not use my two extra votes to convince at least one of them, then democracy be damned—I was captain of this boat. When it came down to it, if anyone left this boat with permanent injury, I would feel responsible. I crawled out on deck and straddled the open rear hatch. "We have four polentas, three grits, three dehydrated dinners, plus two dehydrated beef stews. We _could_ ration this for seven days," I told them, "but I think we should ration it for five." All counted, including the rations of tuna, cheese, and butter, we had roughly thirty thousand calories on the boat—only fifteen hundred calories per rower per day for the next five days. There was nothing left to use as a supplement. Each slice of cheese had to be cut down significantly because of the mold, and about three pounds of peanuts and eight single-serving bags of oatmeal had gotten wet and become rancid over the past week.

It was time to speak. "We are very close to the line, everyone's at a reduced performance, and we are in the most dangerous part of this race," I said. "We could maintain this level of performance for five days, or yet another reduced level of performance for seven." If we tried this and weren't across the line in forty-eight hours, we would still have the option of rationing a little bit more to cross. After making my case, I made a point to emphasize our voting procedure. Would I have the guts to stand my ground if it was three against one?

Dylan nodded. "I'm with you."

I sighed in relief.

Brad cleared his throat. "We have thirty miles to go. That's our focus. Falmouth...is...fucking...gravy. We need to be a team." He was going with the pump-up speech.

Greg sighed as he retreated to the cabin.

"I agree entirely," I said. We needed to wrap this up and get back to rowing. "Our primary goal is and has always been rowing across that finish line. We reevaluate once we get to that point." I wanted everyone to say their piece.

"The wind's supposed to be good tomorrow," Dylan said. "If we don't make it over the next four days, we're not supposed to make it."

"Greg, you good?" I called down to the cabin.

"I support your decision."

—◈◈◈—

No one had ever chosen not to row. Every shift, no matter how we felt, we continued to come out of the cabin and row. If this was not the definition of strength, I did not know what was. The next conversation about food would be whether or not we would choose to row on nothing at all. I could feel the bond that had held us together dissolving. For almost twenty-four hours we had been stuck between twenty-nine and thirty-one miles from the finish line. We had eighty-four hours to make port before we ran out of food.

—◈◈◈—

Greg eyes widened. Thrusting the steaming pot of half-eaten polenta and cheese into my hand, he crashed through the door. Convulsions wracked his body. I pounded the side of the hull in frustration. Scraping the mold off his ration of cheese instead of cutting it away had been a bad idea. We could not afford to have a rower down. He would have to recover enough to row in the next hour and a half. My stomach appeared to be fine, but I had sliced my portion. I made Greg some more polenta, carefully cutting back the mold.

———

The sat phone had one more call left. It was Todd, in the Isles of Scilly. Dylan gave him the latest update on our position, then handed me the phone while I was rowing. "Hello?"

"Jordan?" replied a female voice. It was Rebecca. I had not heard her voice in sixty-nine days. Grand romantic statements were difficult as my interaction had suddenly become the center of the boat's attention.

"It doesn't matter if I see you in Falmouth or Seattle. It's going to be just as good." It was the best I could manage, but that was a lie. Seeing her twenty-seven days from now in Seattle would not be as good as seeing her now, but I could not say that.

I handed the phone back to Brad inside the cabin. Turning to Greg, I said, "That was everything I needed, and everything I didn't." Believing I might still have a chance of seeing her on this side of the Atlantic was too great a risk.

———

We would not achieve David Burch's prediction from the day before; we would not be crossing the finish line by 6:00 PM, not even close. As Greg and I switched shifts, Brad turned to Greg and asked him how he was doing. Greg pretended not to hear, and when we were both in the cabin, he shut the hatch.

"I swear, if Brad asks me that one more goddamn time, I'm going to tell him exactly how I feel. I will not hold back." I stared at him, measuring my response for several seconds. A meltdown this close to the finish line would solve nothing. In the entire sixty-nine days no one had lit into another with the wrath Greg implied. Anger had bubbled precariously close to the surface but had remained contained, expressed through sober conversation and debate. Nothing had been said publicly that could not be forgiven. If Greg broke loose, it would destroy what cohesion and morale was left.

"You can't do that," I said.

He looked at me. His jaw was set. I knew I could not stop him. "Are you asking me as a friend or a captain?"

In twenty months I had never ordered Greg to do anything. I hadn't ordered anyone to do anything. I had requested, pled, collaborated, brainstormed, and divided labor, but never ordered. The only power I had over Greg was what he willingly gave. I felt he had waited too long to express his anger. The time to do that was not thirty miles from the finish line. I saw the rage inside him.

"I'm asking you as a friend first, and I'm ordering you as your captain."

Later I went outside and quietly told Dylan and Brad that no one was to ask how Greg was until this was over.

—∿∿—

Mark and Erinn had spent the day poaching internet outside a deli in front of the quay in town. Their compulsive checking turned into disappointment, frustration, and eventually beer drinking. After having a pint of British cask ale in each of five bars in town, they decided to start again from the beginning. After each pint, they checked the internet, hoping for progress. Nothing had changed. Even if we started making major miles, there was no way we would be fast enough to get there that night. At one in the morning the bars had closed, and Erinn had completed the heroic feat of drinking as much as the enthusiastic British sailors.

She and Mark checked the internet one last time before passing out. Dylan, Greg, Brad, and I sat one mile closer than we had in the middle of their bender.

At the finish line, seventy miles from Falmouth on a flat sea

Chapter 29

—⁓—

The Agony and
the Ecstasy

Day 69

Night had long fallen. After thirty hours in nine square miles of
ocean, I was ready to be done. Greg and I had finished our shift,
and I retreated to the cabin. Greg stood outside—stretching, peeing,
drinking water, and socializing with Brad and Dylan as they made
ready to row. Something had caught his eye, an imperceptible
bubble of lighter-colored night on the horizon. It disappeared.
Fifteen seconds later it reappeared, then disappeared again. The
spot hadn't moved.

"Guys, I think that's Bishop Rock Lighthouse." Greg pointed into
the blackness, and Brad and Dylan followed his line of sight. I stared
at the coordinates for the finish line drawn on the white bulkhead
above me. I refused to believe it.

"That is light," said Brad.

"Definitely a light!" affirmed Dylan.

I poked my head out of the cabin to see for myself. "Where is it?"

Greg pointed northeast. The lighthouse light could not actually
be seen. What he had observed was a small bubble of light created
by the powerful Fresnel lenses beyond the horizon. It was weak but
the light was unmistakable. I began to sing a terribly off-key and
enthusiastic rendition of "My Bonny Lies Over the Ocean" that was
soon picked up by everyone.

"Oh my God, it just keeps flashing at us! It just keeps saying 'there's land, right here!'" said Greg. It was a boost to morale, even though our reality had changed very little: we were still in the ocean.

Greg read the GPS through what I suspected were tears. "49.22.420 north and 7.06.285 west." That was it, the first sighting of the Bishop Rock Lighthouse. He was jubilant. "What a day, what a way to end a tough set of days and begin what could be another tough set of days."

Dylan shoved his oars back into the oarlocks and turned to Brad. "Let's get closer to that light."

Day 70

Little had changed in two hours, but I thought I could see the light on the horizon more clearly. The boat was just over twenty miles away from the finish gate, and it seemed practical to try and get ahold of Mark. The satellite phone had finally died the day before during our last call to David. Our only long-distance backup communicator was the ARGOS tracking beacon tied to our stanchions on the side of the boat. Throughout the journey it had transmitted our location minute by minute. It had four settings: "We are okay"; "We are okay, but need assistance"; "We have an emergency"; and "We are okay, but have no long-distance communication."

—◦◦◦—

It was 5:00 AM. The ARGOS tracking beacon on the *James Robert Hanssen* had just signaled an emergency. *The wankers probably hit the wrong button*, Mark thought. Still, he began to wake the crew.

—◦◦◦—

I moved out of the cabin to get ready for my daytime shift. A wood-hulled turquoise fishing boat floated a few dozen feet away with two men in thick wool sweaters, mouths agape. For a second it seemed as though we had entered the late nineteenth century. Then they pulled out their cell phones and began taking pictures. "Where did you come from?" the younger one asked.

"New York. We're heading to Falmouth."

They stared silently and sized us up. "Well then, welcome to Cornwall!"

———

I woke from a deep sleep to the sound of hell breaking loose. Dylan and Brad yelled wildly, incoherently. An unfamiliar yet unmistakable high-pitched roar of a powerful outboard motor howled. Greg and I scrambled out of the cabin. A black rigid inflatable boat with four people galloped toward us with a rooster tail of wake. Three men and a woman in dry suits pulled up alongside. They looked like space explorers in a B movie. Erinn grinned from ear to ear. Celebratory profanity filled the air as the wake rocked into our boat. Big white letters adhered to the side of the vessel read "World's Toughest Rowing Race."

Mark got right to the issue. Our ARGOS distress signal had terrified him.

"We tried to send the signal that our communication was down. Our sat phone died yesterday," Dylan explained, shrugging in apology.

For a moment it looked like we were about to get some serious chastisement, but Mark's relief outweighed his annoyance. He pulled out his satellite phone to let Woodvale know we were okay. It had taken less than an hour to get to our last position but two hours to find us in calm water. This meant we were a mere 11.6 miles from the finish gate. After reevaluating the RIB's gas supply, Mark decided they would escort us to the finish. Erinn started snapping photos.

In the water, seaweed was more abundant, like a promise of green grass ahead. Surreal tranquility pervaded the smooth slate ocean. We could hardly feel a breeze. Inside the dark thunderclouds a mile away, hot and cold parcels of air began to fall and rise next to one another, generating a long and visible funnel of wind that reached down to the sea, creating a dancing waterspout. In his thirteen Atlantic crossings, Mark had never seen this.

With three miles till the finish and ten minutes till Greg and I went on deck, it was likely that the two of us would have the honor of crossing the line. The tiny *James Robert Hanssen* was about to become the first boat crewed by American-born men to row the

North Atlantic. Our bodies had felt weak for a long time, and under that threat we had made the choice to move. The prospect of finishing made us strong.

Rex, our mascot hidden in the bow for months, was pulled out and tied to the bow, the place he had stood as we passed under the Verrazano-Narrows. Some of his rubber skin was torn and moldy, but his tiny yellow eyes remained fiercely defiant. Greg and I took our position on the oars. Now it seemed the tide would do it for us.

Out of earshot of the RIB, I put four choices before us. When we crossed the finish line, we could take a tow to land; we could continue with a thirty-mile row north to the Scillys; we could continue with a fifty-mile row to Penzance; or we could go for broke, rowing the extra seventy miles all the way to Falmouth. The boat felt light, and we made sure all our camera batteries were charged, ready to document the occasion. Our flags were out and the finish line was ahead of us, nothing more than an imaginary line drawn across the ocean.

———

"We have five hundredths of a minute to go, that's like fifty yards ahead." Dylan interpreted the GPS coordinates. We counted down the last ten thousandths of a mile to 6.27.7° west. "Ten, nine, seven." We skipped numbers—for the first time the boat moved too fast. "Five, two, zero!"

Cheers erupted from both boats. Miles of ocean extended in each direction, and without our GPS we could not have differentiated it from any other calm day at sea. For the first time since New York, we put down our oars without guilt.

"So that's it?" asked Mark.

Greg stood up and put his arms in the air. "That's all there is to it."

———

Each of us gazed into the distance, lost in our thoughts and exchanging huge grins. Head in his hands, Greg wept. The deck was silent save for our sniffles. The *James Robert Hanssen* had rowed the North Atlantic. I realized that now, when people thought about my dad, they would not just think about how he had died at a young age.

Dylan looked me in the eye with fierce and teary confidence. "I think it's the coolest thing you could ever have done." Greg pointed the video camera at my dad's picture. There he sat, still smiling. His beer had not tipped the whole way across. "Cheers, Jim," he said. "The J. R. Hanssen guys," said Brad.

Greg's camera moved to the picture of his grandparents. "Thank you, Grandma. Thank you, Grandpa."

Brad brought out the permanent marker we'd been using to mark our days at sea. He reinked the faded lines of "In Memory of Penny and Mum." "She always thought I was nuts," he said quietly.

———

On the sat phone Mark confirmed with Woodvale that we had in fact crossed the finish line. They asked for a quote, and the guys looked at me. "It wasn't just the four of us that did this," I said. Jim Hanssen had been there too. But it had taken far more than the five of us to accomplish this. More than a hundred names were adhered on the inside of the boat, and over a dozen sponsors were on the outer hull. From donations of a few bucks to tens of thousands in goods, services, and cash, they had given us the privilege of rowing across the ocean. Hundreds had contributed to this journey.

"What do you say now?" asked Greg. It was time to decide just how we would finish this row. North to the Isles of Scilly and we might have a beer on shore that night. Fifty miles to Penzance and we could still get the mainland-to-mainland record. With a tow we would see everybody tonight. Jim Wood and Douglas had changed their ticket last minute and were leaving in two days. We had just over a day to make it to shore. But if we rowed all the way to Falmouth, I might still miss them. I had already made my choice, though, and I knew the others would understand. I cleared my throat: we were going all the way to Falmouth.

"Before we start...," Brad said, with a wry smile. Four gold-and-red packages flashed in his hand: Twix bars. They had been kept safe deep in the boat for almost a month. I had been threatening to eat mine for the past ten days. Now I was glad I waited. It was the first of any sugar we had seen in two weeks. Greg and Dylan were almost in tears at the sight of them. Four tiny tangerines sailed through the air from Mark's boat to ours.

Greg held up a tangerine and spoke first. "Unassisted mainland to mainland. Are we still okay?" No one had torn a peel. Mark shook his head and looked at us like we were crazy. How four tangerines could possibly count as "assistance," he could not fathom.

"You're fine," he replied.

———

The last thirty miles had taken fifty hours. It was as if we now had the ocean's blessing to convey ourselves safely to the shores of England unmolested. We said our good-byes to the RIB crew, and Mark floored the boat back to the Isles of Scilly. Alone on the sea once again, we headed northeast to conclude our voyage in the manner we saw fit.

———

Perhaps our angst itself had caused the sea to whip into froth. Unhindered by that emotion, the miles rolled by with carefree ease into a sunny, amiable afternoon. We made our heading slightly more east than north. Mark had warned us of the strength of the currents around the Isles of Scilly. It was part of the reason that no boats had made it to English shore without touching the Scilly Isles first or getting a tow. David Burch would have been proud, and I wished we had some way to reach him beyond the tiny dot on his computer screen.

In the distance another speck approached at high speed, a big blue-and-white boat, its profile much higher than the RIB but just as fast. A tall figure was standing on the gunwale. She had beautiful, dark brown, curly hair under a trucker hat. It was Rebecca.

I had suspected that if she had found her way to the tiny archipelago, the possibility existed that she would make her way onto a boat. Earlier that night she and Todd had observed the lightning storm that had hit us. We had both looked at the light made by Bishop Rock. We were so close, and if anyone would do it, it would be Rebecca.

Windblown from the ride out, she looked amazing, her skin tan from a summer of outdoor play. She had a broad, bright smile. "I love you!" I yelled.

"I love you too!" She pulled off her cap, showing *The Internationalist* logo on it. A while back, I had jokingly suggested to Nick that he make the hats. In a show of solidarity, he'd done it. Todd filmed with an enormous grin. Three salty-looking men from the Isles of Scilly whooped like schoolboys at the four bedraggled strangers in the rowboat. A smoke flare was lit, adding an unearthly red to the blue-gray world around us. An entire airhorn was emptied in four long blasts.

"What the hell you doing way out here?" asked Todd, looking up from the camera.

"Making history," Greg said casually.

"We just rowed across the ocean!" Dylan called.

"Did you guys finish the race?" asked Todd. It was the shot he had waited weeks for, and he'd missed it. This was a good second best.

"We're done! We passed about an hour, hour and a half ago." I took my gaze off Rebecca and turned to Todd—I knew he had a hand in getting her out here. "Thank you," I said.

"What's the plan?" asked Todd.

"Falmouth," said Brad.

"We're finishing it," I said.

The sailboat Eve *sails out of Falmouth Harbor to cross bows with the* James Robert Hanssen *after seventy-two days at sea.*

—∿∿—

Chapter 30

LAND!

Pray to God, but keep rowing to shore.

—Russian proverb

Day 70, Late Night

Conditions remained calm. It was one of the warmest nights since we left the Gulf Stream. Different configurations of lights danced in the distance, suggesting the variety of boats close to shore. We ate a decent meal and planned to roll into port with an empty boat. By morning, the west wind whipped the waves into choppy five-footers. Around noon, the RIB stopped by, and Erinn got her action shots. Her pictures of the placid water at the finish gate had been for posterity, but they did not capture ocean rowing.

Greg squinted into the distance. "LAND!"

Between the blue of sea and sky, a hazy, light brown band cut across the horizon. Terra firma was not impressive at this distance. It seemed much farther than fifteen miles to the two-hundred-foot cliffs of the Lizard Peninsula. Mark was already making plans for our arrival—late night or early morning. The predictions had begun again. Our fragile imaginations, so recently sated by lighthouse sightings and the image of land, contemplated our exact arrival time in Falmouth.

An ocean's worth of aches and pains emerged from the depths of our muscle fibers. The sight of shore gave us permission to recognize them. The thick wood oar handles and mix of gloves had proved a good strategy: it looked like we would row the entire ocean with seven blisters among us.

Day 71

Afternoon turned to early evening. We had come close enough for the brown band of land to separate into beige beaches and dark rock cliffs, topped with green hills and the occasional plume of chimney smoke blowing east. Seven-foot marine-blue swells rolled us east. Perfect conditions for the next five miles as we rounded the Lizard, but less so as we began rowing the final twenty miles north to the harbor. A white yacht danced in and out of our vision. It was looking for us. Crowded onto its upper and lower decks was what looked like a very full load. The yacht rolled precariously. Greg and I called to Dylan and Brad to come out with the camera; we had visitors.

"Do I know you guys?" Greg called out above the wind.

Everyone was on board except Brad's mother Meg and my own. Given the rocking of the boat, both moms would have felt wretched. Rebecca, having seen us the day before, stayed home and kept my mom company. Marie, Greg's mother, was reconsidering the wisdom of her choice to get on the boat. Linda, Dylan's mom, sat next to Dylan's girlfriend Emily, neither of them letting on if the rolling bothered them. Greg's girlfriend Betsy was also on the boat, eager to get back to solid ground and have Greg on it.

Salvos of "I love you!" were flung across the waves.

Keven Vickers, Brad's dad, beamed at his son. Even in the fading light, he looked healthier to Brad than he had seemed in years. He wondered if his dad had made good on his promise not to smoke while he was at sea. Next to Keven was Brad's Uncle Peter and his friend Chris, who had managed to convince his generous boss a second time for time off. Kathy, the documentary producer, sat on the top deck next to Marie. Todd had not slept in thirty-six hours and was now strapped to the edge of the boat with a lifeline, camera in hand. Dylan's father Ron and Greg's father Dave stood on the aft deck shooting pictures. With our scraggly beards, knit caps, my leather cowboy hat, and our matching yellow-and-red foul-weather gear, we looked like something out of Victorian science fiction.

Jim Wood and Douglas were on the boat too. They had found us at the last possible moment: a half hour later and our boat would have been invisible in the dusk. They had seen me row to England.

Todd turned the camera to get Doug's reaction. Doug clinched his jaw, shaking his head. Todd read the request and turned the camera toward us.

"When are you leaving?" I called, tears rolling down my cheeks. My father couldn't get a flight change. He was leaving tomorrow.

"That's okay. You're here now."

"That's right. I'm here now."

This was my good-bye. "I will see you in New Mexico." It seemed strange I would have to go to a desert to see him next.

"Fair winds," he called.

"And following seas," I said, completing the phrase.

"You make me so proud, so proud!"

The wind continued to rise and the captain of the happy and seasick loved ones turned his boat back to Falmouth, leaving us to our labor. Dylan turned to me. "Let's get you to shore." If we could get in by tomorrow morning, I would see everyone. We were racing again.

—∿∿—

We cleared the Lizard around 11:00 PM. This had been our seventy-first day on the water, and Falmouth was eighteen miles north of us. I no longer had any doubt about our location when the fireworks began—an odd coincidence, like the anniversary of Liberty State Park on June 10, the first day of the race. Apparently the red blasts were a weekly celebration during the summer.

Around two in the morning, the waves built to ten feet and it began to rain. Out of the night the RIB blasted by our bow. The tiny, powerful craft was lit up like a Christmas tree. Mark and a crewman wore their dry suits with helmets and full faceguards to block the spray. One trough separated the rowboat from the RIB as we rode the waves. Mark yelled above the din that he was dropping off a cell phone for us. In a cheery voice he warned us of the Manacles—a set of ominously named rocks just below the surface of the water, a mile off the east side of the Lizard. In the past two hundred years, these rocks have sunk more than fifty ships. He wished us safe rowing, promising to return to escort us to Falmouth.

Day 72, Our Last

Wind was not favorable, but it was not directly against us. We traveled inexorably up the coastline. By morning we had been rowing close to land for twelve hours. Snippets of detail came in gusts—a lone dog barking and the unmistakable smell of a fire keeping one of the picturesque cottages warm. Simon Chalk, the head of the race organization, came out that morning, giving Mark a brief respite. With three ocean rows to his name at the time, Simon knew how we felt.

As the last ten miles of the row dragged on, I made peace with the reality that I would just miss my father and brother. They had come out in the ocean to see me, and that would have to be good enough. We had staggered our shifts since morning so that we could all row together. Greg rowed with Brad until Dylan replaced him. We passed the Manacles in late morning without drama. A lone yellow-and-blue bell buoy was rocked by the waves, ringing a mournful warning of nearby danger. Land encircled more than half of our vision, like open arms waiting to embrace us. Behind us, the sea suddenly seemed overwhelmingly vast and mysterious.

The mouth of Falmouth harbor was close, but it was still several miles away. Todd and Erinn had come out on separate RIBs to film and take pictures. Tour boats brought curious strangers to cheer madly until, like so many inquisitive dolphins, they realized that our futuristic craft was merely a rowboat—the locomotion of which is not particularly exciting to observe. Greg made polenta, tuna, and cheese for the last time. We had a half pound each of polenta and tuna left—no one was enticed to finish it.

By late afternoon the sunshine created metallic filigree on top of the water. Brad finished his last two-hour shift. Dylan had been rowing for an hour and stayed on. He had never traveled to England before. I felt like I could row forever and onward into oblivion. Filling Brad's seat, I turned to Dylan. "We're not standing up until this boat's in Falmouth."

—⁓—

A stiff northwest wind began blowing, adding to the outgoing tide. The combination was making our entrance into the harbor go at a glacial pace. Todd was exhausted but happy. The light was perfect for filming. His phone rang and he took the camera from his shoulder to pick it up. "That was David," said Todd incredulously. "He called to tell me to move to your northwest quarter to block the wind."

Burch had been watching us on the map all morning in Seattle, carefully observing the wind. Seeing the northwest winds we were experiencing, he postulated that even a relatively small craft might create a wind block to make the rowing a little bit easier.

—∿∿—

Field and farmland gave way to a bristling, low, rocky coastline dotted with the battlements of Pendennis Castle, Victorian hotels, and seaside cottages. The mast of a recently sunken sailboat moved back and forth ominously on the rocks with the lapping of the tide. On the lowest battlements my mother was watching with the rest of the family. I could not pick her out in the crowd, but I knew she was there watching the growing flotilla of boats escorting us.

The team stood up, hugged each other, and turned to shore, cheering at the top of our lungs: "All my life I want to be a Logger! Hack! Hack! Chop! Chop!" With each "hack" and "chop," we swung our hands. It was a chant from the UPS rowing team where we had all met, years ago. The shouts of our devoted parents and loved ones echoed across the water. Through the cheering, Greg heard his dad's distinctive whistle. Seconds later, our chant was repeated, led by our parents. By its strength it sounded like they had enlisted a few locals. It was another mile and a half before the dock.

Gliding out of the harbor came a wooden sloop, a classic vessel with a wooden mast, two taut jibs, and gaff-topsail. The boat, with a crew of six, peered curiously at the *James Robert Hanssen* and crossed our bow by less than a hundred feet. On shore, my mother froze at the sight of it: three large navy-blue letters spelled out the boat's name—*Eve*. No one had seen this boat in the harbor over the past two weeks. The likelihood that a boat named *Eve* would ever sail past the *James Robert Hanssen* was slim. That it would happen at the end of a transatlantic rowing trip, less likely still. If my father was looking over us and wanted to get her attention, he had not been subtle.

The tide grew stronger and it took the better part of an hour to make it around the point and into the harbor. Brad had wanted a flotilla; now he had one. Dylan's father Ron paddled next to us in a kayak. A tiny wood boat with an old two-stroke engine puttered up beside us. A woman sat in the bow and introduced herself as an ex-pat from New York. The old bearded man steering brought the boat alongside and shut down the engine. He pulled some oars from the bottom of the boat, put them into the oarlocks, and rowed silently next to us.

Falmouth revealed itself in stages. After the castles guarding the harbor were large docks with industrial cylinders. Beyond this was the stern of the naval auxiliary ship *Monts Bay* in the middle of a paint job. By the time we could see its bow, the town was spread before us. Hundreds of boats of every make and propulsion were scattered around the harbor. The old houses just behind the Falmouth quays were stacked side by side, above cobbled streets and warm pubs.

Left and right, boat horns went off in celebration, and when we passed by its bridge the *Monts Bay* pulled its foghorn in salute. Delighted, we all raised our arms to mime pulling the horn. They gave another short toot followed by a deep long blast. The oars vibrated in my hands. The smell of greasy fish and chips wafted across the water. The crowd began to sing "Row, Row, Row Your Boat."

Rebecca looked out at us from her spot on the orange all-weather lifeboat docked next to where we would pull in, then quietly called down to Douglas on the dock. She told him to stand where she had been so he could catch our line. More than two hundred people had gathered below and above the dock. Dave and Marie, Greg's parents, were throwing rose petals in the water. Dylan put his hand on my shoulder. "I can see your dad watching you right now. I can't imagine how proud he is of you."

I knew this was true. Jim Wood had said this last night.

Dylan and I stopped rowing and the boat coasted slowly. We were rusty on the motions of docking. Awkwardly I stowed my oars, and Dylan pulled us in. Three hours had passed since I'd sat down next to him. He had been on the oars for four straight hours, yet he looked like he could row another four. He kept the boat's momentum to a minimum and attempted a smooth dock in front of our ecstatic audience.

I stood up and scanned the shore looking for my mother, but before I could spot her, I saw them: Jim in his wide-brimmed hat and Douglas, ready to catch our rope. They had been able to change their flight arrangements at the last moment.

The boat moved in, inch by inch. The raucous singing stopped, as if everyone held their breath. I collected the dock rope that had been stowed since New York. It was moldy after a summer in the bow. I tried to untangle it but could not concentrate. Brad took it from me, as I stood useless with my hands on my hips.

"You guys are all so quiet!" yelled Greg. The crowed cheered again as the boat moved closer.

My dad's voice rang out above the others. "Well done! Well done! Nicely rowed!"

Brad tossed the rope to my brother, and he pulled us in. Simon Chalk sprayed champagne and caught the other line, grabbed my hand, and pulled me on shore, into my dad's arms. In seconds I was enveloped by my mother and brother as well. By the time I let go and realized what an ass I had been for jumping out of the boat before the rest of the crew, I saw that each was with his respective combination of parents and loved ones.

Rebecca hung back, smiling, waiting patiently for the ruckus to die down. I stumbled toward her, pulled her close, and wrapped her in my arms.

Dozens of loved ones and almost two hundred people we had never met greeted us on shore. (Erinn J. Hale)

Chapter 31

The Mountaintop

Scones, clotted cream, Cornish pasties, beer, and champagne shoved into our hands, we drank and ate awkwardly, not willing to let go of the food as the hugs were exchanged. Kenneth Cruchlow, the head of the Ocean Rowing Society, was there to make our crossing official. A friend of my father, Nick Howes, and his wife Sue had come down from St. Albans. I had not seen them in years, and they hugged me like a son. A scale was brought out—alas, not a Hanson scale. The four of us had lost a collective 145 pounds, although this physical toll was hidden beneath our foul-weather gear. Mark tied up the rigid inflatable boat and pushed his way through the crowd to give each of us a bear hug. Todd, Kathy, and Erinn put down their cameras as all the emotion and small talk of the summer was exchanged.

I looked up at the bulkhead, suddenly aware we were being watched. A crowd above stared silently down on the loving, hugging, and kissing crowd on the dock. I scanned the faces—all of them strangers. They had waited for hours to see us row into port. "Thank you, Falmouth!" I called out.

One by one we said good-bye to the boat that had been our home for months, feeling somehow sad to leave it alone that night. With our families helping us arm in arm, we stumbled up the gangplank and through the town square. As we passed the single open restaurant, the dining crowd gave each of us a standing ovation. We convened at the house my parents and the Spooners had rented and ate home-cooked chicken and rice (chosen by our mothers for easy digestibility). Nothing was said at dinner about the lack of food. They attributed our skinniness to just another ocean rowing by-product. Currently full and surrounded by more food, I gave the hunger little thought. We could talk about mistakes later in our film interviews with Todd and Kathy. There was fresh fruit, and I plowed through a dozen small sweet peaches with complete disregard for my GI tract. By the time I got to my second huge slice of cake, I wanted to vomit but I pushed through the pain. The gaunt, windblown, and now showered bearded features of my crewmates seemed out of place at a dinner table. I doubted any exotic fabric could hold a candle to the luxury of the new cotton sweatshirt that Rebecca had picked up for me.

That night I slept four hours in Rebecca's arms and woke amply rested. I said good-bye to my dad and Douglas in the dark before they headed to Heathrow Airport. My mother and I took Rebecca to the local airport. Embracing, we kissed. It would be twenty-five days until we saw each other again. I had seen them all for fewer than ten hours, but I had seen them, and for that I was grateful.

Over the next week, Dylan, Brad, Greg, and I floated about the town of Falmouth. Brad's uncle had given him use of an old Land Rover. We wandered—eating, walking, eating—our paths crossing at least once a day at the Cinnamon Girl Cafe. There were so many people and so many things to look at. I got a glimpse of how sailors, fresh from ocean voyages, would feel a class among themselves, utterly disconnected from those who lived on shore.

Greg took control of our message to the media, fielding phone calls and emails at an epic rate. I marveled at his motivation, and I gave what interviews he told me to. Todd and Kathy interviewed everyone save me. I told them we were going to Ireland, to climb Knocknarea, and they could interview me there. I always understood we were going to Sligo after the row. It was not part of the boys' postrow recovery, but they would never think of not going.

—•—

Six days after our arrival, the *Yorkshire Warrior* made it into port. Their families and regiment had come out to meet them. Brad, Greg, and I watched from above the dock. The crew had decided to get a tow in from the finish line. Twenty-four hours before that, Dylan had taken up Mark's offer to take a ride out to get them in the RIB. Bundled in his familiar dry suit and blue knit cap, Dylan returned grinning. His energy and endurance astounded me.

The *Yorkshire Warrior* rounded the corner of the harbor. Their regimental colors, green with a yellow lion holding a flag on top of a white rose, fluttered victoriously. They rowed the last few hundred yards to shore. The crew was wild-eyed, eager, and frantic with affection. It was hard not to see them as a reflection of OAR Northwest six days earlier. We watched from a distance and then went down to congratulate Captain Paul Tetlow.

That was five days ago. Today the *Commando Joe* remained sixty miles west of Bishop Rock. For eleven days we had slept late and gorged ourselves. The idea of being stuck at sea for almost two more weeks seemed incomprehensible, yet they continued to row. Through their VHF radio they communicated via passing ships that they were not planning to take a tow and would try to row into shore. No one was aware that they were running out of food and losing more weight than we had. Woodvale's boat had resupplied them, but the rules dictated that if they did not break the seals on the packaging their crossing would still count as unassisted.

On September 3 they made it to Falmouth harbor, where thirty-knot winds kept them from entering. Undaunted, the crew rowed east another twelve miles to Mevagissey harbor. Less than one-and-a-half miles from shore, the wind and tide kept them from touching land on their own. They forfeited an unassisted land-to-land crossing and reluctantly accepted a tow. A huge crowd waited for their heroes. Until this time, no one knew that they had chosen to row on completely empty stomachs for two straight days. When I saw their victory picture, I shuddered.

Rain or blue sky? This was the west coast of Ireland on the last day of August. Likely we would have both. Despite the climate's natural volatility, I continued to look for proof of Jim Hanssen's presence in a gust of wind or a ray of sun. Beaten and battered on its northwestern slope by the air and water of the North Atlantic, the thousand-foot limestone mound of Knocknarea stood on the largest of two peninsulas in Sligo Bay. In my pocket I brought fire in the form of a newly purchased lighter. I carried a manila envelope addressed to my father, at Knocknarea, Sligo, County Sligo, Ireland. It was a very specific address, considering I was hand-delivering it.

Inside the envelope was a handwritten letter on heavy stationery, kindly supplied by Olive and Michael Quigley—friends who were neighbors of my mother and father more than twenty years ago. For the days we were in Ireland, my mother and I had been their guests. The Quigley house lay a quarter mile from where my mother, father, and I had lived. The rest of the OAR Northwest boys were staying at the home of Charles Roberts, a childhood friend of my father and uncle. Charles and his wife Breda had generously offered their home.

I had written the letter to my father that morning in the Quigleys' study. Detailing our accomplishments over the past months, I thanked him for a safe trip. I acknowledged the emerging confidence that I had gained: I could be the son of both him and Jim Wood— this was not a contradiction. In fact it never had been—it just took me a while to realize it.

But there was more than my letter in the envelope. A rumor had begun in the press alleging a plan to take one of our oars and plant it on top of the mountain. Logistics of hauling a ten-foot stick through airport security aside, the good people of Sligo might take umbrage to a foreigner impaling their picturesque cairn with an oar. An offering from the trip did not seem out of place, however, and before we cleaned and packed the boat for shipment back to Seattle, I had carved a silver dollar–sized chunk out of each oar handle. These I planned to immolate along with the letter.

I could detect a bit of skepticism from the Quigleys toward this neo-heathen ritual. Another possibly pagan tradition I would give a nod to met with more approval. It was common practice for the climbers of Knocknarea to take a stone from the bottom of the hill and leave it at the top. Whether this custom was as old as the Stone Age monument itself or a romantic tradition begun sometime later mattered little. It was what my grandparents had taught me.

Uncle Eric had climbed Knocknarea earlier that year and entrusted to me an almond-sized black pebble from the mountain to take on the row across the ocean. I had stowed the pebble in a small plastic bag in the gear net that hung from the top of the cabin. On our way into Falmouth I had stared at it in a somewhat macabre way, as though it were a piece of my father. While cleaning the boat in the backyard of Mark's picturesque cottage in the Cornish countryside, I lost the pebble among the cleaned and drying equipment. I had spent the afternoon quietly devastated by the loss of the totem. With some mental and spiritual gymnastics, I finally managed to get my mind to agree with my heart that the loss was appropriate. It was destiny that a small piece of the place my father rested now became part of the Cornish landscape—but only if something from Cornwall was traded in return.

Now on the mountaintop, I carried four small rocks from the beach below the lower tower of Pendennis Castle in Falmouth. These brown-and-tan stones, like the carvings off the oar, were Plan B. Armed for the divine end of the quest with four stones, four chips of wood, and a letter to my dead father, my mother and I waited in the gravel parking lot for my teammates and the documentary film crew.

—⁓—

The four of us wore our matching tan sun shirts. We waited for Todd and Kathy to finish preparing the film equipment. I handed each of the crew a rock from Falmouth. Before the hike, Kathy had asked if I would be willing to read what I had written in the letter. I politely refused. After four months I had become much more comfortable sharing the story about my father's death, but I wanted something for myself alone.

We began the climb. I walked in silence next to my mother, ahead of the boys. She did not appear troubled by the cameras or by my decision to invite the filmmakers along. I asked her what she felt my father would think of being included in a documentary, considering we could not ask his permission. "Jordan," she said, laughing, "your daddy was such a ham. He would have loved this." It was not the answer I expected, but with this Jim Hanssen became a bit more human to me. I had never imagined my father with an ego or a hint of vanity. I liked it.

Along the way, we rested among the low stone walls that cordoned off the meadows. We looked out into the distance to the green patchwork of meadows and low rolling hills around us. If a landscape can be both rugged and soft, the west coast of Ireland is it. Beyond the trail, purple heather filled in the skin of the hill. My mom picked a sprig of it. The boys and I moved in loping strides, our legs still weak as our bodies continued to adjust to land. Stepping up hills and stairs seemed to be the last type of strength to return. I looked at the trail and thought of myself climbing the mountain at three years old. As at that time I was too short to see beyond the fences, I studied the trail closely, looking for a memory on the well-trod path.

The cairn, light gray and looming forty feet above us, came into view. It was flat on top, like a miniature of the mountain it was situated upon. Its sides seemed as steep as a rock pile put together with fist- and head-sized rocks could be. We waited for the camera crew. My mom led us up the cairn. I watched out behind her in case she slipped, but she hiked with a strong, steady step. The top of the cairn was covered in grass and dirt in contrast to its looser, rocky sides. Like a Russian nesting doll, another smaller cairn, almost three feet tall, rested on this one. This was obviously where the stones from the bottom were to be left.

Two miles west was the North Atlantic, and the wind blew hard. No one felt like saying much. My mother sat down on the cairn's edge to look north at our old house across Sligo harbor on Rosses Point. The crew looked out into the ocean. With almost an embrace, the wind wrapped our clothing around our thin bodies, revealing bony shoulders and backs. Despite nearly ten days of constant overeating, we had not gained weight yet, but we did look healthier.

Brad put his arm over my shoulder, and I returned the gesture. He had learned a hard lesson that might have broken other people, but not him. If anyone was closest to the spark that created our adventure or the fire that almost destroyed us, it was Brad Vickers. But it did not destroy—it tempered us. Greg harbored the hardest feelings about Brad, but even he had already summed our trials and accomplishment in measured words: "The victory was that the only thing that went wrong was the fact that one guy forgot to pack some food and we got pissed at him for that."

—∿∿—

The mood was different from the first time I had climbed Knock-narea twenty-one years earlier. Not somber, but quiet and contemplative. "We all underestimated the Atlantic a bit," Greg had said earlier that week. Many things had happened in the past eighteen months. Good things and some things that would need time to understand or forgive. This was the place to start. We had a record, and we had won a race, but I was not exactly sure what any of it meant. I liked what Jim Wood had to say: whatever it was, it could not be taken away.

"I think I may need some strong-backed lads to block this wind," I called over to the boys, and we converged on the cairn on top of the cairn. Of course, the moment we had hit shore, the inevitable tide of our separate lives began pulling us apart—it was only natural. I knew there would be events back home that would bring us together, but by then our other lives would have grown too clamorous for us to connect like this. I needed my crew one last time. Now that we were on Knocknarea, I hoped they understood.

The top of the cairn proved a bit too windy to light the envelope, so we moved the operation to the base of the small cairn. My mom kneeled next to me. Dylan, Brad, and Greg balanced on the loose rock and formed a wind block. I stuck the lighter into the envelope, trying to start the fire from the inside. It clicked several times, but nothing happened. The wind was still too strong. I twisted the paper inside at Greg's suggestion and tried again. It worked.

The wind fanned the small blaze, engulfing my letter and the wooden oar chips. The flames licked black ash into the air. It burned longer than I expected. As the fire began to die, my mother dropped in the sprig of heather. "He was so young," she said, wrapping her arms around me. The fresh plant curled and blackened but did not burn, and the remains blew away with a gust.

If I expected emotion and tears to overwhelm me, they did not. With the last of the flames burned out, I stood with my mother. She gazed at Rosses Point. I looked at the kind faces of the three men I had rowed across the ocean with. "There it is," I said, and opened my arms.

The four of us embraced until one of us said something that made us all laugh. From my breast pocket I pulled out the sand-smoothed beach stone from Falmouth and placed it on top of the cairn. Brad, Greg, and Dylan followed my lead, and we balanced four small rocks on the top of the mountain.

Victory!

Epilogue

Throughout the book it is no doubt clear that a lot of our motivation was based on breaking records, and for the sake of narrative I simplified some things. Here I will briefly go into the nuance.

When I speak to people I tell them we spent seventy-two days at sea. It was actually seventy-one days, three hours, twenty-two minutes, and thirty-five seconds. For simplicity's sake, I count ourselves as finishing on our seventy-second day at sea.

The Guinness World Record we hold for the row is the first team to row unassisted from mainland USA to mainland UK. I am proud of this record and recognize its value for other expeditions.

I am sure you remember the tangerines tossed to us by Mark Terry at the finish line. A black-and-white definition of this event could tip the balance from an unassisted mainland-to-mainland row to an assisted row. I worried about this for several years until I came across a definition by Gerard d'Aboville, the first man to solo row both the North Atlantic and the Pacific. In a letter to Kenneth Crutchlow, adventurer and Executive Director of the Ocean Rowing Society, Gerard writes:

> *Assisted rows are:*
> *Those, where the assistance is planned, represented by a programmed supplying or by an accompaniment.*
> *Those, where the assistance or other form of direct help, although not planned, is organized by the rower or by his family/friends. So, here, it is a response to a "request of assistance" (in the maritime legal meaning of the word).*

Unassisted rows are:
Those done in autonomy, and in which pure luck of a not
requested meeting can be the occasion to send some news or
to receive superfluous goods.

Whether you define four tangerines as "superfluous goods" or not will dictate how you define our row. I leave it up to you.

—⁓—

In the summer of 2010 the granddaddy of ocean rowing records was broken. The boat *Artemis*, captained by veteran ocean rower Leven Brown, with an equally experienced crew of Ray Carroll, Don Lennox, and Livar Nysted, rowed from New York to the Isles of Scilly in forty-three days, twenty-one hours, twenty-six minutes, and forty-eight seconds. This was roughly eleven days faster than George Harbo and Frank Samuelsen, seventeen days faster than the Dutch four, and twenty-seven days faster than us. They became the fastest boat to ever row the North Atlantic. It was an epic feat—one I would totally be lying if I said I wasn't a tiny bit jealous of. Then again, it would be a very different story without those extra days.

—⁓—

When we got home all four of us scattered. Greg had the best plan—in that he had one. The week he returned he continued his prerequisite courses in physical therapy. Four years later he graduated from the University of Puget Sound's graduate program in physical therapy and is now practicing. Dylan began working for the Northwest Marine Trade Association, the organization that puts on the Seattle Boat Show where we lived for ten days rowing over forty miles a day. Brad began working for Larry Schildwachter at Emerald Harbor Marine. Six months later they happily switched jobs. Dylan worked for Larry for four years and is in his third year of law school at Seattle University. Brad became director of the Seattle Boat Show but has moved on and is planning his next adventure. Both of them have put up their oars for now and become avid sailors.

That first year back was hard for all of us. As we recovered, each of us suffered various levels of depression as well as several months of binge eating brought on by the rationing. Multiple overuse injuries kept us from being as active as we all would have liked. We each gained back our weight in spades—me most of all. I gained sixty pounds by December 2006, roughly thirty pounds over my average weight.

—⁓—

In December of 2008 my Grandpa Stan died. He had become sick just before Christmas. I read him our logbook at his bedside. I really wanted him to know the story, and I wish I could have read this finished book to him. My family, a mix of Hanssens, Woods, Fischers, and Persons, climbed up another mountain. This was Picacho Peak in Las Cruces, New Mexico, about a mile behind my grandparents' home. Grief came with the comfort that few people had lived so richly. We remembered him in quiet tones, scattered his ashes, and drank red wine from plastic cups in his honor. I think about my death and wonder about all the places I would like my ashes to be scattered. But I'm in no rush.

In the years since the row I have, for better or worse, defined my life by the next adventure. I still live in the same house, renting out rooms and working odd jobs so I can live cheaply and plan another expedition. I have bicycled from Perth to Sydney, circumnavigated Washington's Olympic Peninsula in an open dory with Greg, and walked and canoed several hundred miles of the muddy Rio Grande with my brother, and most recently circumnavigated Vancouver Island in the *James Robert Hanssen*. I want to live the next adventure and then I want to write about it. I'm not sure if my path has been the most effective toward this goal, as I struggle between what I dream to do versus what I think I should do. It's a lifestyle that has been hard on my relationships. I struggle to come to terms with how to balance the desire for stability with the desire to wander.

At this writing I am preparing for another ocean crossing. Why? Quite simply: I'm not done with rowing oceans yet. Nor did I feel like I wrapped up the last row in the way I should have. In the winter of 2012/13, if all goes according to plan, I will row from Africa to South America in the *James Robert Hanssen*, again part of a team of four. The boat has been completely overhauled. Our focus has changed from records and speed to education and research. I learned a lot from rowing the ocean. When the inspiration to row hit a second time it seemed like we could use our boat to do more than row. Using more advanced communications and scientific equipment I believe we can bring a powerful and dynamic teaching tool into the classroom. Our mandate will be to document anything exceptional and send information back. Ocean rowboats are strange. Few platforms have such a long range combined with a slow pace so close to the water. There is a lot to see, and I want to see more.

We are at a new stage in our lives—a bit more experienced and saddled with a bit more responsibility. OAR Northwest has a title sponsor for the first time, the Canadian Wildlife Federation. We are thrilled to have them on board, and it will be exciting to see where this will take us. I hope you will follow the adventure.

About the Author

Jordan Hanssen was born in Mobile, Alabama, in 1982 and was raised in England, Ireland, New Mexico, and Washington State. His family imbued him with a love of travel that has taken him down rivers in Thailand in bamboo rafts and cycling through the French Alps. In 2006 he rowed from New York to England: this book tells his story about that experience. Since then he has canoed hundreds of miles of the Rio Grande and rowed all over the Pacific

Dr. Ian White

Northwest, most recently finishing a circumnavigation of Vancouver Island by rowboat. He is planning another ocean row from West Africa to South America in winter 2012/13. When not traveling or writing, Jordan lives in Seattle and struggles with the endless task of renovating his 98-year-old house. To learn more about OAR Northwest and Jordan's rowing expeditions, visit oarnorthwest.com.

OTHER TITLES YOU MIGHT ENJOY FROM THE MOUNTAINEERS BOOKS

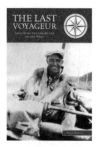

The Last Voyageur: Amos Burg and the Rivers of the West
Vince Welch
A fascinating biography of the quintessential Western adventurer and river runner

Spirited Waters: Soloing South Through the Inside Passage
Jennifer Hahn
Adventure travel and natural history intersect in this solo kayaking narrative.

A Long Trek Home: 4,000 Miles by Boot, Raft, and Ski
Erin McKittrick
A young couple hike, paddle, and ski from Washington State to the Aleutian Islands.

The Tecate Journals: Seventy Days on the Rio Grande
Keith Bowden
A first work from a new voice that is parts gritty, elegant, and contemporary

Walking the Gobi: A 1600-Mile Trek Across a Desert of Hope and Despair
Helen Thayer
The bestselling author's story of crossing Mongolia's Gobi Desert